English for
Gifted and Talented
Students 11–18

English for
Gifted and Talented
Students 11–18

Geoff Dean

Los Angeles · London · New Delhi · Singapore

SAGE Publications Ltd
A SAGE Publications Company
1 Oliver's Yard
55 City Road
London EC1Y 1SP

SAGE Publications Inc
2455 Teller Road
Thousand Oaks, California 91320

SAGE Publications India Pvt Ltd
B 1/I 1 Mohan Cooperative Industrial Area
Mathura Road,
New Delhi 110 044

SAGE Publications Asia-Pacific Pte Ltd
33 Pekin Street #02-01
Far East Square
Singapore 048763

Library of Congress Control Number: 2007936001

British Library Cataloguing in Publication Data
A catalogue record for this book is available from the British Library
ISBN 978-1-4129-3604-0
ISBN 978-1-4129-3605-7 (pbk)

Typeset by Bookcraft Ltd, Stroud, Gloucestershire
Printed in Great Britain by The Cromwell Press Ltd,
Trowbridge, Wiltshire
Printed on paper from sustainable resources

With great thanks to those colleagues who contributed so importantly to the English committee I chaired for the National Academy of Gifted and Talented Youth (NAGTY) 2005–2007:

Peter Thomas, Paula Iley, Erica Glew, Simon Wrigley, Mike Jones and Louisa Shorland.

Contents

About the Author

Geoff Dean began his teaching career in an English department of a boys' grammar school in Northamptonshire, before becoming Head of English at an upper school in Suffolk, where he was later Senior Teacher and Head of Sixth Form. He became Deputy Head at Sharnbrook Upper in Bedfordshire, from where he moved to become English Adviser (later Inspector) in Oxfordshire in 1988. He was appointed English Adviser to Cambridgeshire in 1997, then moved on to Milton Keynes in 1999, where he is currently a School Improvement Adviser.

Geoff has taught English, drama and media studies, and is a senior examiner for AQA A level Media Studies. He is the former Chair of the National Association of English Advisers. He has written five books: *Challenging the More Able Language User* (1998/2001), *Teaching Reading in Secondary Schools* (2000), *Teaching English in the Key Stage 3 Literacy Strategy* (2002), *Teaching Grammar to Improve Writing and Reading in the Secondary School* and *Improving Learning in English* – all published by David Fulton. He leads many courses and speaks regularly at conferences, mostly on his specialist subjects of 'more able English pupils' and reading. He is an avid film fanatic and an enthusiastic reader of texts for young people.

Acknowledgements

The author would like to acknowledge permission given to him by: Simon Wrigley – for use of his reader self-evaluation questionnaire; Professor Ron Carter and the English department of Nottingham University – for use of materials from the LINC project.

Introduction

While writing the first words of this book, I listened to a radio news item about the government requiring secondary schools to identify and register their most able students, and I reflected on how dramatically trends have changed in education. Only twenty years ago, many English departments would have been very uncomfortable with the idea of making special provision for their most able students. The suggestion of separating 'the sheep from the goats' was anathema to the prevailing English teaching sensibilities. Now, all schools are expected to identify their more able students, and forward their names to a national database. More able/Gifted and Talented students have moved to centre stage.

Yet many more able students in all subjects in secondary schools are still at some distance down the 'pecking order' of most teachers' priorities. Anybody carefully analysing the lesson or unit planning of the vast majority of teachers, in all phases of education, will recognise a universally practised pattern. This process involves establishing learning activities and ideas for the majority of students in the group as the first step, followed by setting up appropriate support for the students who are least confident and the more challenging learners, with – almost as an afterthought – some final attention given to the two or three most able in that class. This procedure for designing lessons has become so commonplace that it is now wholly accepted as unproblematic. But it does not have to be the prevailing template, and challenges to that orthodoxy are considered more carefully in the chapter on learning in English.

Until quite recently, there was usually little argument about which students qualified as 'more able' in English. They were those who read widely and often, without prompting, and/or those who wrote fluently in an engaged manner, possibly arguing and speaking at a sophisticated level. They were mostly the young people who went on to become members of English A level groups, and many eventually read English as a university subject. Yet, as English teachers have begun to acknowledge and embrace a broader range of texts as eligible for study in their classrooms, including those which they realised had more to do with the ordinary lives of their students, so the criteria for identifying students who might be thought of as 'more able' in language-related activities have also grown. Teachers are increasingly noticing students who are assured and confident film-makers and film viewers; young people in their classrooms who are 'expert' computer games players, with a strong knowledge of complex narratives; avid and critically discerning readers of graphic novels; young people who are wholly at home on many areas of the internet, who might even run their own websites and regularly 'blog'. These activities have simply never been validated as being part of 'official' English by most English departments, yet they are patently pursuits relying on high levels of language and communication skills. I believe that teachers of English have to review fundamentally the formerly established historic characteristics of their supposed more able students, and adjust the programmes they currently offer in their classrooms.

Throughout this book I shall refer to the 'more able'. I believe this to be a more accurate, comfortable and helpful term to describe the sorts of student dealt with in this context. The government in England insists on labelling these young people as 'Gifted and Talented', although they are referred to in other terms in other parts of the British Isles. 'Gifted' in the government's view (apart from all the other loaded implications associated with the word) is understood to refer to those who have *academic* capabilities beyond age-related norms; while 'Talented' is a term applied to significant abilities in the *creative arts*, *physical* and *musical* arenas. This crude differentiation presents a multitude of problems for teachers of English, who would not, for instance, easily be able to classify an act of narrative fictional writing in the 'academic' or 'creative literary arts' categories. Just as difficult would be the demarcation of students who might thoroughly understand a scene from a play, and then perform it magnificently. 'Gifted' or 'Talented'? Why have two labels, when one will do? I also believe that teachers in Wales more often refer to these students as 'more able', so there will be groups who identify more closely with such a designation.

In actuality, this book is not concerned with the 'gifted' or 'highly able', those young people of exceptional ability that most teachers come across rarely, if ever at all, in their maintained school classes (although some of their needs could be met by including them in the sorts of suggested activities). My attention is fixed firmly on those students who are – by very simple definition – more able than the majority of their chronological peers. Some students have to be 'more able' than the others. 'More able', in this context, means those students who are notably comfortable in, and display high attainment in respect of, more demanding language, linguistic and literary studies.

How to Use this Book

This book makes a number of fundamental claims:

- The more able students in any subject should be of major concern to their schools, and their special needs should be understood, clearly articulated and addressed.

- More able students in English should be studying and exploring in curriculum contexts well beyond the programme required for National Curriculum compliance.

- More able students in English should be capable of increasingly independent study and determining and pursuing their own areas of further learning.

- More able students in English are not merely those who attain highly in examinations and tests, or who will go on to study English in Higher Education settings.

- More able students in English will flourish in circumstances where they are encouraged to 'personalise' their programmes of study.

- More able students in English require access to more than the traditional ways and resources of demonstrating their understanding, knowledge and skills, which is usually through writing.

- Paying proper attention to more able students raises many difficult questions for teachers and schools that cannot be answered with simple solutions.

- Paying proper attention to the needs of the more able students is an important step in raising expectations, and ultimately the academic standards of all students in the school.

In the early years of the twenty-first century schools are, at last, being asked to pay proper attention to their more able students:

- The government requires all mainstream maintained schools to register the names of the students identified as more able to ensure that schools will not allow them to underachieve and to ensure that they gain appropriately high examination and test grades.

- Ofsted includes in its criteria of what distinguishes a successful school that the school should ensure its more able students succeed at levels commensurate with their abilities.

- Enlightened school senior managers recognise that 'inclusion' can only become a reality if all groups of students are genuinely provided for in an equitable manner.

- Personalisation is increasingly being regarded as a necessary direction for educational development, and the more able are being regarded as that group of students who will truly benefit from experiments with this approach.

Yet there are few secure and straightforward sources of advice and support for teachers confronted with the requirements which stem from these new demands.

This book is designed to raise an agenda and set some focused issues in respect of more able students in English, and offer some practical advice, based on work undertaken in classrooms and through discussion with many teachers and students. The matters raised are designed to enable teachers of English to review their practices in the light of changing demands on and in the subject, and – ultimately – to bring about improved achievement in a range of respects for more able students.

The ideas for this book have grown over a number of years of involvement with more able language users and their teachers, in Foundation Stage, primary and secondary schools. Some ideas have emerged from working with more able students directly in their classrooms, others have developed as a result of devising and presenting many courses across the country since the early 1990s. As a local authority adviser during that period, I have enjoyed the opportunity of working alongside English departments in two shire counties and a unitary authority, in a very wide range of school backgrounds, in both the maintained and independent sectors. I am immensely grateful to a large number of teachers who have allowed me access to their students, and have also contributed to, challenged and amended the ideas I have shared.

More recently, I have enjoyed the privilege of chairing, first, the English 'think tank' at the National Academy of Gifted and Talented Youth (NAGTY) based at the University of Warwick, and, subsequently, the English working group drawn from the original body of 'thinkers'. These groups have been prepared to consider a radical agenda, capable of providing a much changed programme of English studies for more able students different from the historical orthodoxy. In the partly frightening and partly exciting context of subject content change and developing school reorganisation (e.g. personalisation), English teachers have a significant opportunity at this time to think beyond the many constraints and strictures that have so invasively damaged the professional involvement in and broad infrastructure of the subject since the late 1980s.

After years of perceived, or actual, increasing centralised prescription of the contents of the English curriculum and associated methods of teaching, schools are now being encouraged to think more creatively. Primary schools received documentation in 2004 entitled *Excellence and Enjoyment*, urging review and reconfiguration of their learning programmes, and secondary schools are beginning to respond in similar ways. A few schools are in the process of radically adapting the organisation, accessibility and content of their provision, yet even the most cautious institutions recognise that some form of change has to be acknowledged and that all groups in the school will benefit from more focused attention. There are many suggestions about how some of those changes might be effected in different settings.

The reader will also find advice on identification of more able students and the sorts of responsibilities and tensions such identification inevitably brings about. Identification should be a shared strategy in English departments; all the teachers involved should be confident that they have agreed criteria for recognising the wide range of factors that might qualify a student as 'more able'. If the ways of 'looking out for' the more able are collaboratively agreed, there is a stronger likelihood that the individual members of the English staff will be conducting lessons in similar ways capable of supporting students to the best possible achievements. Departments not so attuned might well overlook students who do not comply with the idiosyncratic personal definitions of each separate teacher.

Schools now have access to huge amounts of data about their pupils, and it is possible to 'track' all students from the earliest days of their formal education until their final examination results. More importantly, it is possible to see whether individual students have made the sorts of progress they should have done, relative to their former achievement, and that they were truly capable of making, at all stages of their education – especially in a 'core' subject such as English. Yet there are areas of possible progression in English not covered by examinations and tests, and teachers should be aware of ways of growing and making academic advancement in this subject beyond numerical data.

Of course, any advice about improving the conditions, opportunities and support for more able students will not just be about raising the levels of achievement of that single group. Improvements and positive change for those young people will also influence and bring about change for *all* other students served by the English department or faculty. The much quoted maxim, 'a rising tide raises all boats', is very relevant in these circumstances. If teachers begin to think differently and more ambitiously about what their more able students might achieve, they raise the stakes for all other learners. The mainstream students can also be re-motivated and excited by seeing their more able peers bring about impressive outcomes of their study, and approach their work in a variety of unusual ways. This book, therefore, is not exclusively about the more able. It has been written to challenge a number of long-standing and apparently unproblematic routines and practices that have been common in English for up to five decades.

Personalisation is one such example of an area of development worth exploring with more able students which has also the potential to be employed with all students in time. Because personalisation requires teachers and schools to work in unfamiliar and, in some circumstances, uncomfortable ways, it is an initiative worth exploring first with smaller groups of students who are capable of regulating their own affairs and who will probably be more highly motivated.

Finally, this book does not claim to be exhaustive on the subject of providing for the more able in English. There are hundreds of teachers in schools across the country, already offering very worthwhile and challenging programmes of study for their ablest students, who will never employ some of the suggestions and ideas contained here because they have far better suggestions and practices of their own. It is a feature of the subject that it is capable of being approached equally effectively from a number of possible dichotomous directions. My approach is, unapologetically, mostly from a stance that Brian Cox, in his attempt to design the first national English curriculum, named as 'cultural analysis' (a view emphasising a critical understanding of the world in which children live, the possible ways of making meanings and the values they convey). I hope, however, that what is contained in these pages will contribute to significant discussion in some English departments and lead to focused and searching questions being raised about current provision, which might contribute to its improvement.

Further reading

Cox, Brian (1991) *Cox on Cox: An English Curriculum for the 1990s*. London: Hodder & Stoughton.

How to Use the CD-Rom

The CD-Rom contains pdf files of resources from the book separated by chapter. You will need Acrobat Reader version 3 or higher to view and print these pages.

The document is set to print at A4 but you can enlarge pages to A3 by increasing the output percentage using the page set-up settings for your printer.

Throughout the book, you will see this CD-Rom icon used. This indicates that there is electronic material available on the CD-Rom.

All material on this CD-Rom can be printed off and photocopied by the purchaser/ user of the book. The CD-Rom itself may not be reproduced or copied in its entirety for use by others without permission from SAGE Publications. Should anyone wish to use the materials from the CD-Rom for conference purposes, they would require separate permission from us. All material is © Geoff Dean, 2008.

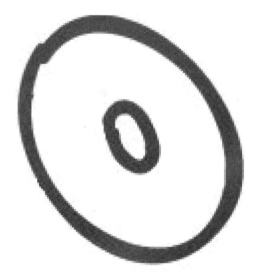

CD-Rom Contents

Chapter 2

Graphic Novels

Blogs in the Classroom

Chapter 3

Before devising your policy, do you have in place ...?

Outline Plan for School Policy for More Able/G&T Students

Achieving the Best for More Able Students In Milton Keynes Secondary Schools: Advice to Schools – Spring 2007

Using Bloom and the Taxonomy of Learning in English

Chapter 4

Alternative English Curriculum Model

Rethinking the English Curriculum in Secondary Schools

Long-term English Planning

Long-term Planning Strands for Progression

Medium-term English Planning

Progression and Challenge for More Able Readers

Qualities/Characteristics of the Reader

Good Readers

Reading is ...

Themed Book Suggestions

1

Why it is so Important to Address the Needs of More Able Students in English

> **What this chapter is about**
> > possible opposition to more able identification
> > why it is important to identify more able students
> > the eight 'P's of identification
> > ways of identifying more able students
> > problems of identification

Undertaking to deal effectively with the more able students in school involves extra work, sustained energy and genuine long-term commitment. Yet teachers who have understood these implications and are still prepared to provide appropriately for that group will be instrumental in bringing about a changed student body with a refreshingly new approach to their studies, capable of achieving improved results, making any extra effort thoroughly worthwhile. Teachers should find their commitment and investment of extra time being rewarded with increased professional enjoyment and success.

Possible opposition to more able identification

As increasing attention has been paid to more able students in the past decade, there have been arguments in some quarters that they are not a deserving separate group. Attending to the needs and requirements of its more able, the argument continues, is an essential duty of any school staff, because schools exist to meet the needs of all their students. Good schools will, therefore, naturally subsume the needs of the more able within a properly formulated and scrupulously applied whole-school inclusive teaching and learning policy. Such a position would certainly be true of an ideal school situation, and ought to be the ultimate position to which all schools should aspire, but it is a long way from the reality that currently exists. Until all students are fully and appropriately provided for, it will be necessary for some degree of special attention to be paid to vulnerable minorities, including those students considered as 'more able', to ensure that they succeed at the appropriate levels.

A few critics, such as Professor John White, formerly a teacher of educational philosophy at the Institute of Education in London, make stronger cases about the possible dangers of social engineering hidden away in the particular provision for the more able.

I would claim, however, that British education has for too long failed to pay proper attention to the needs of the more able. A number of reasons have been proposed to explain this neglect, including a propensity to be embarrassed by and feel awkward in the presence of those who make a show of intellectual superiority. As David Miliband, a former Minister of State for Education, remarked in a speech in 2004:

> Until five years ago, bright students were too often confronted by the very British mentality which says it's wrong to celebrate success, and worse still to actively encourage it. The bright student was too often embarrassed by being labelled a smart-alec. (Miliband 2004)

In some institutions, able young people are derided and insulted by a few of their peers with names such as 'boff' or 'nerd' and unprintably worse epithets, as ways of underlining their status as unacceptable outsiders. Some students, running this gauntlet daily, have to be very courageous or thick-skinned to withstand such provocations. In such circumstances, only the truly unusual or determined manage to resist a very common urge to conform to their peers and continue, against the odds, to demonstrate their true abilities. These situations may not be universal, but sufficient numbers of teachers I meet on courses recognise these particular difficulties when considering supporting their more able students to suggest it is a major national problem.

The dominant mode of teaching in the subject English from the late 1960s has been increasingly inclined towards a mixed ability model, where all students in a class were treated 'equitably'. Unfortunately, 'equally' was too often misinterpreted as 'the same'. A great many schools see it as their first duty to support those students who encounter problems with reading and writing in the secondary school, and, in the main, have been less prepared to ensure that an appropriate and commensurate level of challenge and support was made available for those who cope very successfully with the English curriculum. In fact, teachers were often grateful to have a proportion of more able students, who would – they sometimes reasoned – require *less* attention. More time would then be available to devote to the members of the weaker group.

Some teachers also showed an antipathy towards the establishment of an elitist 'upper' group. Such identification was occasionally regarded as morally objectionable and clearly 'wrong'. I know that these perceptions existed, because I saw them at first hand in my early days as an LEA English Adviser. Occasionally, the situation was twisted in quite absurd ways. The more able students were invited to extra-curricular clubs or societies, and even residential out-of-school events, where their abilities led to more advanced and challenging tasks and activities, but that same greater ability was not actually acknowledged or provided for appropriately in the mainstream English lessons.

The least satisfactory provision was made where more able students were correctly identified but the result of identification was that they were expected to do more work. They might be required to write longer pieces or read 'harder' novels, as if doing 'more of the same' was the best way of 'getting better' – whatever 'getting better' meant in those circumstances (often not very precisely defined). If there is one solution that more able students always hate, it is being asked to do more activity or study than their peers, as they believe that they are being punished for their greater ability.

Why it is important to identify more able students

The eight 'P's of more able provision

Pride

First, identification should involve a degree of *pride*. Everybody should want to be proud that the department is determined to encourage and make progress with its very best students. The school should be proud that it has a department capable of addressing the needs and ambitions of its very best students. It should also be proud of its able students and prepared to celebrate the unexpected and extraordinary things they might well be capable of performing. The students, in turn, should be proud that they are being purposefully challenged and have the opportunity to demonstrate their most creative and personal attributes. They should want to share their successes with others, and expect the respect and admiration of their peers. Parents should be proud of the quality and richness of the work their children produce, and the extra buzz that they feel as a result of the level of commitment and interest of those young people might then have in their studies.

Other ways of representing this exigency are developed in the following further seven 'P's.

Personal

It is the core purpose of every school to ensure that every student has his/her particular unique needs met, and that every student achieves at the level of which s/he is capable. Any provision that fails to achieve less than this goal is a serious shortfall that needs immediate and continued attention. Somewhere, in every school prospectus, there will be a statement claiming that every student is 'valued' and entitled to this treatment. It must be regarded as more than a merely rhetorical statement, and parents should be in a position to ask about seeing the evidence of such claims when paying their early visits to the school. The recent government commitment on this matter is very deliberately entitled *Every Child Matters*.

Professional

Every teacher should want to be part of the apparatus by which their students achieve at their highest possible level. It should never be sufficient to be 'satisfactory', merely keeping students occupied at unsatisfactory levels of attainment. The research of Jean Ruddock and her colleagues at Cambridge University School of Education shows conclusively that too little attention is paid to many students' former learning and achievement in the two years following transfer to secondary schools, and a large proportion of more able students claim that they are bored and dissatisfied with the early years of their secondary schooling (Galton, Gray and Ruddock 2003). Giving serious consideration to the requirements of the more able students, and recognising the sorts of academic feats of which they are capable, is a way of raising teacher expectations, not only for this identified group but also for that of their peers.

Much importance is ascribed these days to 'assessment for learning' and a fuller consideration of that idea is pursued in detail in other parts of this book. Yet a broader interpretation of the term 'assessment for learning', meaning all that is known about the student beyond mere statistical details, will require teachers to seek detailed knowledge about the strengths, interests and range of qualities their learners bring to the classroom. All those minutiae are a very helpful prerequisite for the fuller learning process.

Political

Many more able young people leave or are kept out of the maintained education system in England because their parents perceive that they will not be adequately provided for in their local secondary school. Of course, not all able students come from middle-class backgrounds with the capacity to make alternative school arrangements, but state school teachers have to face up to this realistic challenge and prove not only that more able students can be appropriately catered for in maintained schools but also that they will achieve as well in public examinations and in their future lives. Teachers in maintained schools in certain areas have to challenge the mythology that only independent schools can fully satisfy the needs of the more able, and impress on parents who can afford to purchase a private education that it will be money wasted. At the other end of the social scale, teachers may have to raise the expectations and horizons of their able pupils, who may be hampered by a lack of ambition.

Progress

All students should be able to make progress and improve in any educational enterprise they are pursuing, whatever their academic starting point. I have regularly asked Heads of English, for instance, how they intend to improve the reading abilities of their most able readers, and been met with blank expressions in response. This is rarely an area of progression given any real attention. Yet there is never a ceiling in learning; and no learner ever reaches the end of a learning journey. There is always more to learn, or other ways in which to explore and apply what is already known. Carefully paying attention to the next stage of each student's development should always be uppermost in the minds of teachers dealing with more able students. Teachers should, as a matter of course, be asking themselves 'what next?' in respect of any student's development. Students should also be asked where they wish to take or further exercise their learning, and so give greater weight to the influence and power of their own student voice in this enterprise.

Prospective

The young people covered by the scope of this book could go on to be the potential leaders, professionals, decision-makers, producers and creative ground breakers of tomorrow. They may include the authors, poets and dramatists of the next generation. Our society needs them to be as skilled, confident, well prepared and open-minded as possible, and, just as importantly, as aware as possible of their latent potential for achieving true fulfilment in their future lives. Early and fully attentive identification of these students can lead to the design of appropriate and well-designed courses, capable of yielding wide-ranging benefits. But such provision should not be exclusively for the benefit of the more able; we want all our young people to be fully, ultimately, what they are capable of being. Raising expectations for the more able should lead on to raising expectations about all young people.

Pleasure

More able students in English should be able to derive huge pleasure from their studies; they have the potential to involve themselves deeply and to establish coherent links across their curriculum-based activities and their own interests. If their teachers know these students well, and acknowledge that they bring into their schooling involvement and expertise from other areas of language and linguistic enterprise, they will be in a better position to devise uniquely focused, alternative approaches to the courses of study, incorporating those pursuits in their planning for learning. A 'one size fits all' attitude is becoming increasingly challenged in course design, and it is particularly inappropriate in respect of the more able. There should be many ways in which an area of learning can be shared by a number of students, but separate pathways to the learning outcomes should be constructed to suit individual interpretation.

Paradigm

Paying the proper attention to the more able students in the class can also have hugely positive effects on all other students. When more able students are confident and comfortable, they are more likely to offer models of response and creativity that might not come as easily to their more mainstream peers. They will demonstrate superior feats of insight or suggest directions of thinking from which their classmates could derive extra stimulus and guidance. Teachers often adjust their own expectations of what all students can achieve when they are able to experience confident, empowered students working at their most fluent.

Personalisation

A further topic – personalisation – could be added to this list at this point. It is a significant notion with the capacity to absorb and have impact on the whole of the rationale outlined above. Because of its emerging important potential, it will be considered in greater detail later in this book.

Possible ways in which more able students in English might be identified

More able students in English can be identified in a number of ways. It is always better if teachers use a range of identification procedures to give the process greater credibility, and do not merely depend on isolated incidents (although these should never be overlooked, as we will explore further). The major procedures include the following.

Tests and examinations (and value added)

In an age when tests are proliferating, teachers are expected to examine carefully the data they provide. English teachers in secondary schools should have access to a bank of results from tests already conducted on their students, from the age of 7, before they arrive at secondary school: Key Stage 1 and Key Stage 2 national test results, as well as a group of 'optional' (although most schools now employ them) tests administered at the end of years 3,4 and 5. In the secondary school itself, most English departments will conduct their own 'optional' tests at the end of years 7 and 8, and enter their students for the national end of Key Stage 3 test. (A few schools are currently moving towards providing a slightly changed arrangement for more able students, by entering them for the Key Stage 3 test at the end of Year 8.) Students consistently achieving high results, particularly in English/literacy, across this wide battery, from the age of 7, would, quite clearly, appear to be probably 'more able' and deserving of appropriate provision. The national expectation of attainment in the core subjects (English, mathematics) at age is 7 is Level 2+, so children achieving Level 3 at that stage are already slightly in advance of their peers. Level 4 is the expectation at age 11, and the more able should be achieving at least Level 5. At Key Stage 3, aged 14, the expectation is Level 5. More able students should be achieving Level 7, or an 'exceptional performance' award.

Secondary schools have long experience in using the Yellis (**YE**ar **11** Information **S**ystem) prediction test exercise of potential student achievement with respect to GCSE. This has been capable of identifying students who should attain the highest grades at age 16, but until the adoption of personal targets this information was not always sufficiently well followed through to full achievement. That and similar systems have recently been supplemented by the Fischer Family Trust data, which makes predictions of students' future results relative to previous performance. English departments these days really do have a substantial bank of data about all of their learners, and should be able to align that statistical information with what they know about the individuals they encounter on a regular basis in lessons, to bring about appropriate outcomes at the end of each Key Stage.

In too many secondary schools, however, students who have achieved Level 3 at KS1 and Level 5 at KS2 fail to go on to achieve appropriately at age 14, or to achieve the best possible results at GCSE. The skill of interpreting the statistical data about students is still relatively new in many English departments, and the notion of 'value added' (being able to demonstrate that students have actually benefited from their education in their current school) is still not universally understood.

While this book was in preparation, the government announced plans to review the use of end of Key Stage tests. Pilot trials have been proposed to explore whether more able students should sit these tests at earlier times than their mainstream peers. There might be superficially attractive reasons for schools to adopt this approach, but I believe there are also a number of less obvious disadvantages which require careful consideration before important decisions of this sort are taken.

Recommendations from primary teachers

Children in primary schools might not always do themselves justice in tests, and a few may even be sufficiently intimidated by the testing situation to perform badly in those formal settings. Youngsters may also display skills and talents not necessarily recognised by the testing regime currently used in schools, and these could be wholly overlooked without effective transitional communication. Strong networks, through which this type of information passes, should be established, where possible, as an instrument of good transition. Occasionally, secondary school teachers do not trust and recognise the judgements and recommendations made by their primary school colleagues about particular individuals. Trust and effective sharing of criteria and student information must be firmly established to overcome these possible disruptions to good transition.

A few transition issues require very sensitive handling. It is possible for a child to be identified as more able in the smaller setting of the primary school, whereas at transfer to secondary school that child's ability is not viewed so positively, and it may not even be included on the new school's programme. Parents and students can be mystified and upset that a student might be regarded as no longer 'able' or 'gifted'. Schools should be fully prepared to explain carefully the rationale behind such decisions. A small number of schools also choose not to inform parents that a student has been identified as more able. In circumstances where previously a parent has been strongly involved in a proper three-way partnership (child–parent–school) to support the progress of a more able learner, it can then be baffling to be excluded from the process.

Parental recommendation

Parents know their children better than anybody else, and a parental recommendation should always be taken seriously. A few parents make inflated and unsubstantiated claims about their children's abilities but these should be treated with proper respect, even if, ultimately, the school does not agree with the parents' assessment. In most instances, where parents feel sufficiently moved to approach the school to discuss their child's ability it is because there has been a sense that the child is not being fully challenged, and the prospect of such a visit might have caused the parent much discomfort. Schools and departments with robust and secure policies in place will be in the best position to explain to parents why positive identification has not been made in those instances where the school has a different perception from the parent. Yet, it is possible that the school has not offered or provided circumstances in which the student has been able to demonstrate their very best characteristics, and such parental prompting could bring about opportunities through which the teachers see the student in a changed light.

Student nomination

I once witnessed a Year 9 student inform her teacher, at the end of the lesson, that she had just read *Wuthering Heights* and needed someone 'to talk to about it'. The teacher had no idea that this student was reading books of that difficulty, or that she had an inclination towards a critical interest in such texts. She quickly reassessed her views about this young lady as a result, and consequently began to challenge her more directly. Some students feel moved to share with their teachers other areas of expertise about which the teachers would, otherwise, have no idea. These skills could be manifested in activities which are not usually validated by the school, so opportunities for discovering these special or different abilities should be part of the English department's 'conversation' with all its students. There may well even be lin-guistically based areas of interest in which a few students are more 'expert' than their teachers, and the potential for discovering these abilities also needs planning into that English 'conversation'. Only by operating a policy of valuing what the students bring to their lessons, keeping an open mind, and being constantly on the lookout for the unexpected, will teachers truly make it possible to discover the true range of students likely to be classified as 'more able'.

Teachers' perceptions and observations

This is the most important aspect of identification. Tests and examinations, however much significance they have for the educational establishment, will never provide the most advantageous and supportive circumstances in which the most able can be expected to flourish. A few more able students have been known to regard tests as a waste of their time, and they have deliberately not performed well in them, as a reaction.

English teachers will regularly claim, with some justification, that the nature of their subject allows them to make closer relationships with students than teachers of any other subject. There is good evidence that they do talk more fully to and with their students than other teachers, and occasional instances of students' written work cover content of a personal and intimate nature. The subject also places high regard on the exploration of feelings and development of emotional response as part of its core purpose. It is possible for teachers, working in this context, more easily to notice small, subtle details of their students' character and personality, not evident to teacher colleagues in other subjects.

A student may occasionally display evidence of greater ability in the classroom situ-ation than might be registered through examinations or tests. This is particularly true of students who are very confident speakers, or skilled in drama, as these char-acteristics are rarely identified in English tests, which mostly depend on developed writing attainment. This same constraint can also work against students who are sophisticated comprehenders of textual meanings, but find it much easier to articu-late their observations in oral discourses than in written ones.

In their interactions in the classroom setting, teachers should be prepared to dis-cover characteristics in their students that have not been transmitted through other identification procedures.

Warning

Most able students are disinclined to demonstrate that greater ability unless they have worthwhile circumstances in which to display their accomplishments. If the tasks they are assigned are boring, unchallenging or commonplace, few students will respond with the energy and enthusiasm that might lead to 'more able' outcomes. Similarly, students not formerly recognised as more able may well show flashes or momentary incidents of greater ability in reading or writing or spoken discourses but not present these characteristics regularly across the whole range of meaning-making activities. These young people should also be monitored, and be encouraged to work in ways that could lead to the more regular demonstration of their superior skills. The potential of students, given favourable conditions and the right sorts of monitoring and advice, should be a foremost consideration of all teachers of English.

- More able students are not likely to want to explore the full extent of their abilities unless the contexts and motivation for their work are sufficiently strong.

- Being 'able' in English is not a state at which all students arrive in one identifiable stage by a particular age: it can be closely associated with a student's maturation. The ability to attune to and recognise the power and effects of language might not be understood by some students until they have experienced certain emotions or life experiences which give those notions real force. These extra abilities are likely to develop over time, and at different stages of schooling. A particular text, an inspiring teacher or working in a new way can be amongst the causes of students presenting quite differently developed qualities of response and communication. Even though a student has not been identified as more able in the primary school does not mean s/he might not qualify as more able at a later stage. Identification should be open-ended and ongoing .

- More able students in English flourish best where the teachers are:

  1   looking out for more able students at the time of primary–secondary transfer;

  2   continuing to identify and support instances of greater ability through Key Stages 3, 4 and 5;

3   providing stimulating, motivating study capable of resulting in excellent, open-ended outcomes;

4   dedicated to ensuring more able students improve their skills and abilities.

Problems associated with identification

A few students may be reluctant to acknowledge their true abilities in English for a number of reasons. Not everybody is comfortable with being 'labelled', or the extra attention that accompanies identification and monitoring. The following issues should be understood and respected by teachers.

Natural shyness or diffidence

A few young people are really unaware of their talents, or think that what they are capable of is not very 'special'. They need to be supportively shown how their own attributes are better than those of more average capability, and can be further developed.

Lack of self-esteem

This is not quite the same as the first characteristic listed, as these students lack the confidence to push themselves to the top level. They need help to become more confident and to see the benefits of linking up with others of similar ability.

Fear of ridicule

Some students are unwilling to be thought of as 'able' because they will be associated with a group of their peers regarded as 'anoraks', 'geeks' or 'boffs' – or even worse, unprintable, terms of abuse. Boys, especially but not exclusively, are sensitive to this negative peer pressure and find it hard openly to live up to their teachers' expectations. Such prevailing attitudes throw a heavy responsibility on the school to help sort out the ways students regard themselves and others in a wide range of contexts, not just in terms of ability.

Michele Paule, who lectures on Gifted and Talented provision at Oxford Brookes University, points out in an English magazine article that able students

> may be considered as a group who have traditionally lacked a positive 'collective story' or identity. Their portrayal in the media has traditionally been negative, via, for example, such characters as Eugene in the film *Grease*, 'Plain Jane Superbrain' from the early days of *Neighbours*, Millie in *Freaks and Geeks* through to Hermione in the early Harry Potter novels and films. (NATE 2006)

Laziness and/or lack of organisation

A few potentially able students either cannot be bothered to attain the expectations about them, or lack the organisational qualities to make them a reality. Occasionally, more able students are not being deliberately lazy when they claim that the truncated version of a task they have submitted has fulfilled all the requirements: they can be literally correct. They sometimes have to be convinced about why work should be of a particular length or quantity, when their abilities allow them to submit material more sharply perceived or understood, in shorter or tighter form than that of their peers. A few students, in the past, have perceived that being regarded as 'more able' means having to undertake extra work, which they resent more than any aspect of the process.

A dislike of the subject

As strange as it may seem, a few students, who are very capable coping with the demands of the subject, do not much enjoy what goes on in lessons. They might, for instance, not enjoy reading books or gain any pleasure in writing, and are unwilling to make progress at a rate commensurate with their potential abilities. Teachers will have a difficult, but necessary, communication with these students, attempting to 'win' them back to the subject, although increasing focus on providing a 'personalised' programme could go some way to alleviating this dilemma.

A dislike of, or lack of involvement with the curriculum

The sorts of skills and interests of some students might simply not be met in the English departmental programme. Their talents could be better manifested through activities such as moving-image study or production, drama or ICT. Links and bridges need to be constructed between their particular areas of expertise or interests and the mainstream content of the curriculum, to allow them to transfer skills and qualities in alternative areas of interest into the mainstream curriculum, possibly by acknowledging their parallel interests in different ways.

A dislike of the ways of working

Some able students will not, for instance, like the pace of their English lessons, as they are capable of making much faster progress than their peers. They might not like spending weeks studying a text, such as a novel, when they have already made relationships with other texts, not being considered. They might not enjoy writing, but would be prepared to make more interesting presentations of their insights and understanding through other media.

Conclusion

Ensuring that more able students are

1   willing to be recognised as 'more able';

2   prepared to live up to the expectations of identification; and

3   ready to accept the responsibilities of being regarded as 'more able'

clearly depends on knowing the students extremely well, having a suitable degree of mutual trust and the continuance of appropriate mentoring and support over time.

Further reading

Galton, M., Gray, J. and Ruddock, J. (2003) *Transfer and Transitions in the Middle Years of Schooling (7–14): Continuities and Discontinuities in Learning*. University of Cambridge Research Report No. 443.

Paule, M. (2006) 'Gifted Identities in Popular Culture – or what Clark Kent could learn from TV.' *EnglishDramaMedia* (Sheffield: NATE), January: 7–11.

2

Who are the More Able in English?

What this chapter is about

In this chapter advice is offered about identifying able students in English:

> more familiar able students
> students who do not comply with the traditional stereotypes of able students in English
> according to the National Academy of Gifted and Talented Youth

Easily identifiable able students of English

Identification of able students in any subject is not a finely honed, scientific procedure. But there are a number of common features which enable teachers to quickly recognise those who might be thought of as 'more able'.

Those students who are very obviously 'more able' often

- are confidently articulate and talk to adults with ease;

- read, make good sense of and enjoy difficult and complex texts without being urged;

- write well with some flair across a range of text types, understanding appropriate contexts and approaches, and the possible audiences of the work – although a few have very developed skills in writing very specialised texts, such as poetry;

- remember ideas and facts easily;

- are interested in problems, and can often see more than one solution, making connections more quickly than their peers;

- engage deeply with particular aspects of their work and may develop their interests independently;

- are curious and question their experiences;

- may well have developed expertise in a specific area of the subject, such as science fiction.

More broadly, English teachers asked to name their more able students do not usually have much trouble reaching for straightforward criteria by which to construct such a list. The eligible students usually display some or most of the following, slightly tongue-in-cheek characteristics:

- **motivation** – they are seen as the 'keen' and 'eager' students, absorbed in their work and ready to engage with it. They comprise a high proportion of girls (fewer boys seem to qualify, as they are not thought to be as interested in reading and, particularly, reading fiction) who can be easily recognised by carrying a copy of the current novel, seeking spare moments to engage with it whenever possible.

- **attitude** – more able students show very positive approaches to their work in English. They are readier to put their hands up and participate in lessons more often, and prepared to share their insights and ideas with enthusiasm. They complete and hand in their homework on time, sometimes doing more than expected. Their reading habits take them outside the normal syllabus, and they are likely to be regular library users and book borrowers. A few might write stories and/or poetry independently, and visit the theatre when they are able.

- **skills** – they read with real fluency, mostly making full sense of text on immediate contact, and are able to call on a wide repertoire of nuances and intonations in their understanding. They quickly see into the author's intentions. Their writing is sophisticated and mature, with good structural solidity, employing an impressive vocabulary, often experimenting with new words, seeking precision. They are confident talkers, and unselfconsciously use talk to explore and feel their way around issues, concepts and ideas.

- **achievement** – these are the students who are likely to be awarded, or already have achieved, A* and A at GCSE, and might well be on course, after two years of studying English at A level, to achieve an A grade at GCE. Most will go on to university to read English, or other book- and ideas-based subjects, such as law and philosophy.

A subject-specific view

In school settings where teachers have been regularly used to working with more traditional curriculum approaches, and where specifically addressing the needs of the more able students is still not fully developed, the following list, most of which I prepared for the *Key Stage 3 National Strategy, Framework for Teaching English: Years 7, 8 and 9,* would still be relevant for identifying and considering the implications of able secondary students.

Being more able in regard to language and literacy skills usually refers to that small group of students who enter secondary school each year:

- capable of demonstrating close reading skills and attention to detail in texts;

- aware of nuances of language;

- as fluent and confident readers, with defined tastes, and engrossed in reading;

- with developing incisive critical responses, demonstrating greater pleasure and involvement in language-related tasks than most other students;

- having developed the ability to read between the lines, and to make good connections across texts and within texts;

- usually able to articulate their intentions and choices in writing;

- recognising the intentions of other writers;

- most importantly – able to reflect more carefully on the sorts of language and linguistic engagements they encounter.

Not all able students will demonstrate equal capabilities in all aspects of English. An impressive reader may not be as skilled in writing, for example, and many able students find safety from the anxieties brought on in an anti-intellectual culture in silence. They may not all be reading 'harder' books, or writing accurate lengthy pieces of writing. Success may come in the form of penetrating wit, divergent thinking, delight in language or in-depth responses. Stereotypes should be avoided in the search for ability.

These students usually, however, are a teacher's dream. They come willingly to school, are mostly interested in lessons and often produce work (and homework) of a high quality. They might undertake projects of their own volition and value a teacher's time and involvement in those enterprises. They are regularly to be found in the library, or in a quiet space about the school, immersed in a book.

Identifying students who do not fit the 'more able' stereotype in English

The world of language activity has changed hugely during the previous decade or so, however, and continues to expand inexorably:

we – teachers as well as students – live in a society that is more fully and insistently textualized than anything people have experienced in the past ... it is impossible to deny that language and other semiotic systems and their associated media of communication have in the course of history multiplied and penetrated more and more deeply into our daily lives. We are at present, like it or not, the most mediated human beings ever to exist on this earth. (Scholes 1998)

Until the late 1980s and early 1990s, the work of most English departments in English schools was almost exclusively concerned with the study of literature – printed in books. A few teachers had begun to widen their repertoire of study into other textual areas – newspapers, television, video and film, for instance – and were urging their students to explore more broadly what a language-based curriculum might comprise. If the programme in any school is firmly focused on book texts, and the principal medium of communication (and the proof of any learning) is through students' written outcomes, then the bulk of accepted success criteria will – not unreasonably – be considered only in those terms.

As the scope of English has increased in its sweep during recent history, there has been a huge increase in the textually based enterprises possible to incorporate into English studies. The proliferation of university courses broadly associated with English, such as Media Studies and Communications, in that period offers some sense of the broadening field involving language and other semiotic interests. Equally significant has been the growth of practical, hands-on skills involving language, literacy and other communications knowledges. Not all of these areas of interest have been integrated into English studies in school, and a large proportion of students may well feel that their particular areas of absorption and engagement are not validated in school terms, and therefore they do nothing to share with teachers or other appropriate adults their involvement or achievement with such activities. Schools may simply not know what their students are truly capable of – or how well they are performing in activities and fields not thought worthy of attention by the school.

More modern preoccupations of able students in English

A large proportion of able English students can still be identified from the more standard sorts of checklists described above. Many of them continue to read and enjoy challenging word-based texts fluently and with real flair. A considerable number write with ease and convey difficult ideas and other material convincingly. Some talk confidently and communicate well in spoken form.

Yet modern more able students in English may well have significant interests in and be very expert in the following textual areas.

Graphic novels

These texts are hardly a modern phenomenon, having been available in their present state since the 1970s, but built on traditions stretching back beyond the Second World War. Indeed, huge numbers of them arrived in ships' holds as ballast in the 1940s and 50s, causing a massive moral panic at the time.

All good bookshops have a graphic novels section, but few English teachers visit them. They are still viewed by large sections of society as no better than comics: valueless and not worthy of attention. This representation of graphic novels would not, however, be recognisable in mainland Europe, where they are regarded as important works of art capable of being compared alongside their word-only counterparts. A few, such as Alan Moore's and Dave Gibbons' *Watchmen* (Titan Books 1986/87), Will Eisner's *A Contract with God, and other Tenement Stories* (Baronet Books 1978) and the Pulitzer Prize-winning *Maus 1* and *Maus 2*, by Art Spiegelman (Pantheon Books 1986 and 1991) have become regarded as important literary works, with many notable serious admirers.

Nevertheless, whether approved or not, they have a large following and fan base amongst young people. (Indeed, it could be argued that they are probably partly admired by this age group precisely because they are so strongly condemned by many adults.) Their devotees understand the ways the pictures and words work together, they are skilled at being able to see how the representations of various points of view in the illustrations contribute to the meaning, and they recognise and explore the, often, multiple narrative devices at work in the text. They also know well the styles and characteristics of the individual writers and artists, and can point to what they regard as the obvious differences between them. There is often a brisk trade in swapping and borrowing. These aficionados speak about these works with the same insights and knowledge as their teachers do of the sorts of texts included in the 'official' literary canon.

In conversation with English teachers, I rarely meet any who know much about these texts. One or two younger teachers have developed an interest in these works, and show the same dedication to them as their students, but they are remarkable exceptions. English teachers should be aware that some of their 'readers' may well be very involved with graphic novels, and encourage them to talk about them, and bring their well-developed skills into their 'official' English studies as they would any other form of fictional narrative reading.

Film-lovers and film-makers

The recent explosion of digital technologies has transformed the ability of ordinary people to become media producers. Just as the spread of the internet has brought about the possibility of anybody with a computer becoming a 'publisher', so has it also encouraged all sorts of prospective film-makers to distribute their independent examples of moving-image work to millions of others, in ways undreamed of twenty years ago. The video camera, once a clumsy, expensive and rare luxury, has become a hand-held everyday household item in many homes, and video-making is possible on massive numbers of mobile telephones.

While reading of words is still hugely important in preparing young people for life, and most able students will have experienced a wide reading programme from their earliest days, books are far from being the sole means or medium through which students will have discovered much about language and life. Most will also have absorbed a huge range of film texts, either at the cinema, or most likely, at home on television or on video or DVD. Most students will own considerably more video tapes and DVDs than books, and these resources may well be regularly replayed, either solitarily or in changing social groupings.

As individuals and in groups, young people are interested in the process of making moving-image pieces – either in the style of film-makers they admire – known as *hommage* – very frequently, particularly the work of Quentin Tarantino – or, some-times, attempting completely new ways of looking through a camera. With editing equipment readily available on home computers (Windows Movie Maker comes as standard on their Microsoft Office package and i-Mac is a constant resource avail-able on Mac computers), it is also possible for young people to capture sequences of professionally made film and then to re-edit them, as well as processing their own material.

Unless an English teacher has already encouraged some developed work around film-making or film editing, there is little reason why that teacher should have any idea that some students may be experienced in this area. I have known groups of boys in their mid-teens who have made their own very creditable versions of *The Lord of the Rings* in their holidays, while their schools have remained completely unaware of the varied range of skills these lads displayed. Others have been moti-vated by animation films that have impressed them, trying out a variety of tech-niques for themselves, pushing their technologies to the limits, sometimes coming up with wholly new sorts of texts, or original hybrids. Lord Puttnam, the former film producer and champion of new 'literacies', reminded a media conference in 2006 that young people with modern, reasonably cheap digital technology, can achieve more sophisticated outcomes than the BBC was capable of bringing about less than a decade before.

Computer gamers

Search for 'computer gamers' in Google, and immediately access to five million 'hits' will be established. It is a massive area of interest, and large numbers of able stu-dents are just as keen on playing these games as any other teenagers. Some play very seriously indeed, and regularly subscribe to magazines and access sites online to research the rules and subtleties of their favourite games. One or two even write their own versions.

These games are very sophisticated constructs, and are being taken seriously by a number of education institutions, notably the Institute of Education in London. Dr Andrew Burn and his colleagues are exploring in their research, amongst other related topics, 'The semiotics of computer games and relation of computer games to literacy and media education'. Whilst some sections of society might dismiss computer gaming as, at best, a waste of time (and despite most English teachers' grudging acceptance of the teaching of film, they still regard interest in computer games as a step too far), there is a growing body of academic interest in the ways that playing them contributes to and improves students' literacy skills and knowledge. At Parkside College, a media specialist school in Cambridge, younger students are expected to construct their own computer games for themselves, on Mission Maker, a game-making platform, as a natural part of the English/communications syllabus, as part of their early skills training.

Anybody aware of their complex narratives and the sophistication of the ways that computer games can develop in a range of different possible directions, will not be surprised that more able students are drawn towards these activities. They are far more than entertaining side-shows. Some students enter the world of their games in exactly the same way that many readers 'lose' themselves in works of fiction. Devotees of these interactive texts need to be recognised in school, given opportunities for their interests and pleasures in them to be articulated and recognised as particularly skilful in an area of literacy understanding. Three English teachers, Don Zancanella, Leslie Hall and Penny Pence, explore the valuable lessons they learned about playing these games in chapter 6, 'Computer Games as Literature' in Andrew Goodwyn's valuable book *English in the Digital Age* (Cassell 2000).

Bloggers and other multi-modal areas of growth

Blogging was an unknown art until very recently, and like many new developments made readily available through computer and internet use, has blossomed to become a major international communications medium. According to the internet encyclopaedia, Wikipedia:

> A blog (a portmanteau of web log) is a website where entries are written in chronological order and commonly displayed in reverse chronological order. 'Blog' can also be used as a verb, meaning to maintain or add content to a blog.

> Many blogs provide commentary or news on a particular subject; others function as more personal online diaries. A typical blog combines text, images, and links to other blogs, web pages, and other media related to its topic. The ability for readers to leave comments in an interactive format is an important part of many blogs. Most blogs are primarily textual, although some focus on art (artlog), photographs (photoblog), sketchblog, videos (vlog), music (MP3 blog), audio (podcasting) and are part of a wider network of social media. Micro-blogging is another type of blogging which consists of blogs with very short posts.

> As of September 2007, blog search engine Technorati was tracking more than 106 million blogs.

Some students who are reluctant writers in school will be very happy to participate in the blogging experience, and may even have developed blogs of their own. Whereas they might be reluctant to write much in the school setting, they are much readier writers in this context because they believe that through this means they will find like-minded and sympathetic audiences, some of whom will want to respond directly.

These skills and enthusiasms will probably not be known by the teachers of the young people involved, however competent they might be in any medium. In the main, only the very newest recruits to teaching will have much inkling about these preoccupations, and actively look out for such accomplishments.

Other computing and digital technology skills

A large proportion of the current secondary student population is completely at home with computer technology. Unlike the adults born before 1990, who have had to assimilate computers into lives where patterns and routines were already established before these technologies proliferated, today's young people have grown up surrounded by differently structured communications artefacts. More able language users are regularly more able users of the available technologies, enquiring and bold in their relationships with computing resources, taking in their stride new and regularly proliferating programs and hardware.

They do not think twice about multi-tasking, or engaging with a number of open screens on a computer – simultaneously communicating with friends and strangers in 'chat rooms', conducting research through a variety of websites, playing a game of one sort or another, while possibly also writing out some homework. These learners are used to reaching for the computer to discover facts, links and prompts for a multitude of requirements. They make extraordinary connections between different sorts of digital devices, enabling them to 'talk' to each other in ways that make working easier. These are a generation who naturally 'read' a wide variety of textual materials in ways their teachers and parents do not manage as easily – using hypertext facilities and linking devices quite natural to them. Many are experienced in using chatrooms to explore quite challenging topics, while others are used to sharing all sorts of biographical details about themselves and others through programs, such as 'MySpace'.

A few able learners will have developed impressive presentational skills by mastering complex programs, such as Photoshop, where they have gained real talents in manipulating and adapting images. They will have explored the many potentially engaging features of programs like PowerPoint, possibly linking image to music or spoken commentary. I have seen examples of really powerful textual analysis presented through PowerPoint, where the images and word and sound combined in ways that added far more to the meaning being conveyed than any essay, however 'thoughtfully written', could ever achieve.

Drama and the speaking arts

Not all more able students in English will necessarily be excellent writers. A few find other ways in which to express their thoughts, insights and understanding, and a popular alternative form of communication is drama. Some young people show from an early age the confidence and skill to step readily into someone else's shoes, and to take on a role. Others develop those abilities as they move through adolescence, becoming keen observers of the lives of others, and quickly able to discern how a character in a play should be portrayed. These students need opportunities for role-play to be found in classroom activities such as 'hot-seating', where they can be questioned 'in role', as a real or fictional character. Students who attain highly in drama do not always seem to achieve in the same way in English. The two departments should be aware of the other's outstanding students and be prepared to support and extend the skills these young people bring to these different lessons.

A number of students also have the potential to shine in **debating** and **public speaking** situations. It is unlikely that most students will encounter these particular activities outside the school context, unlike many of the areas of experience listed above. To ensure that everybody has a real opportunity to show their prowess in this skill, the school will need to organise occasional debates and induct their students in the etiquettes and procedures of these undertakings. With the increasing attention being given to student voice in schools, and the growing power of such institutions as the School Council, and the greater use of students to host visitors to the school, there should be areas outside normal lesson time where young advocates and confident speakers can be quickly recognised and be properly developed.

An holistic view of identification from the National Academy of Gifted and Talented Youth

The Academy has, during 2005 and 2006, concerned itself with surveying the subjects of the curriculum, exploring the issues of identification to formulate advice to teachers. The sub-committee charged with considering what characterises 'more able' students in English began from the following position in a paper entitled 'Key Characteristics of Gifted Learners in English – Cognitive and Communicative Dimensions of Gifted and Talented Pupils in English'. The term 'Gifted and Talented' (G&T) is a government requirement in this context, and should be seen as interchangeable with the phrase 'more able'.

The English group considered assessment for learning: identifying hierarchies of attainment. G&T attainment is defined in holistic terms which may apply at all ages, and not only in relation to speaking, reading or writing. In response to the broadening of the potential English curriculum in more modern times, as described in the sections above, the criteria adopted in the following documentation reflects that breadth. What is likely to distinguish many of the most able is a cognitive ability that may show itself in thinking before it shows itself in other ways, and sometimes in relation to stimuli other than texts:

Gifted learners in English are capable of:

1   **Responsiveness**: natural and ready responses to a broad range of familiar and unfamiliar ideas/language/situations;

2   **Communication**: tentative and/or confident communication of ideas and responses to and in a broad range of ideas/language/situations and roles;

3a   **Referencing and interrogating**: making connections e.g. comparisons, contrasts and contextual sitings across a broad range of ideas/texts/situations;

3b   **Probing, questioning and challenging** the implications of a broad range of ideas/texts/situations.

Having established the grounds in which identification might be conducted, these general features are then filled out a bit further and given greater precision in the following **High Level Descriptors**:

1(i)   Responding to familiar and unfamiliar texts in ways which demonstrate critical understanding and insight, using conceptual frameworks, recognising contextual influences;

1(ii)   Understanding of intended audiences, authorial purposes and the ways in which these may affect presentational choices.

2(i)   Ability to reach well supported and convincing judgements;

2(ii)   Prepared to sustain an independent point of view;

2(iii)   Where appropriate, can produce a precise, mature style of thought/speech/writing or enactment – or an independent style exploiting irregular or non-conformist thought/speech/writing or enactment;

2(iv)   Respond in a variety of appropriate media in elegantly crafted, well constructed, economical, original, imaginative, rhetorical or playful ways.

3(i)   Adapt and synthesise what is understood from a wide variety of ideas/texts/situations/enactments in a variety of ways;

3(ii)   Adopt attitudes/ideas/perspectives not their own, showing ability to empathise with and manage different ideologies and value systems.

This way of regarding more able students in English was deliberately devised to invite English teachers to think beyond the usual assessment apparatus, most commonly provided by QCA during the past decade or so. English teaching, like all other areas of the curriculum, has become – not surprisingly given the huge weight attached to such judgements – too dependent on describing student attainment in an inappropriate shorthand of 'levels'. The NAGTY English group thought their suggested areas of consideration would allow English teachers to make judgements on the government-based criteria, but then to move on and away from such constraints.

This framework was also meant to allow the involvement and engagement of students in activities beyond the more usual, commonplace reading, writing and speaking contexts. It is a model for the twenty-first century, recognising that developing technologies will play an increasingly influential role and require teachers to think differently about the accomplishments and outcomes of their students, and to re-think the relationships between broader definitions of reading, writing and speaking and listening. It, necessarily, employs a very dense language for describing the more able in English.

Many English departments will recognise the level of challenge to their own practice that is contained within such a framework, and respond accordingly. Where teachers of English have already begun to recognise how important it is to meet the needs of the most able students, this apparatus will offer a further stage of development.

The implications of identification

Teachers determining to discover who their more able students might be will be committing themselves to extra work and responsibility as a consequence. A large number of issues flow from such an engagement, including:

- consistency of identification;

- a register or record;

- monitoring.

Consistency of identification

The department will need to agree on a common set of criteria for identification. This will mean careful and precise preparation for accepting that more able students are a genuine responsibility of the department, either in a whole-school approach, or because the department has decided autonomously that it must act in accordance with current national practice.

The government, through the Gifted and Talented Education Unit (GTEU), has issued two very helpful documents – the Institutional Quality Standards audit and Classroom Quality Standards audit – which might be useful for departments in conducting some of their preliminary approaches.

While it is usual to nominate a member of staff to conduct and supervise the business of administering the recording and record-keeping of the more able group, published shared agreement about the sorts of judgements being made will be necessary, particularly for new or recently qualified staff. This process might mean showing examples of individual students' work to colleagues, or even making enquiries about their attainment in other, related areas of the whole school curriculum (e.g. checking ability on drama, or even other subjects in which written or other presentational features might be relevant to progress in English, such as the humanities).

A register or record

Schools will treat this administrative device in different ways, and it is not the purpose of this book to tell schools what to do. Yet I believe that it is vital for teachers to recognise that the record, of itself, is not the real point of registering more able students. It should merely be the starting point of what is then carried out to ensure that these students make progress at properly commensurate rates. The register or record should be the means of specifying the focus of individual student development and progression: each more able student is unique, and their only real connection is the extent of their differences. It must be possible to track how students have moved forward by referring to the register. A 'register' is a double-headed device: on the one hand, it will record the areas of advanced accomplishment demonstrated by more able students; on the other, it will plot a projection of what that able learner could be capable of achieving as a result of the most supportive facilities.

The National Academy of Gifted and Talented Youth describes 'high achievement' as the outcome of 'potential' given the appropriate 'opportunities' and 'support', coupled with student 'motivation':

$$\text{potential} + \frac{\text{opportunities}}{\text{support}} + \text{motivation} = \text{high achievement}$$

The school will need to recognise the potential, and then supply the opportunities and the support. Whilst the student should be expected to contribute the motivation, the school can play an important part in encouraging that quality by establishing interesting and challenging units of study. One of the issues bedevilling the establishment of a register of more able students in the past has been to do with those who qualify for the register: should schools record those who have already attained certain high levels of performance, or should they also include those students that they believe capable of greater achievement given appropriate and sustained support? The latter group may not be the obvious qualifiers, and including them in the register will call on more capacity and resources.

Monitoring

Having identified the students likely to benefit from a programme aimed at the more able, it should then be the duty of the teachers in the English department (or those allocated to conduct such business) to ensure that genuine progression ensues. Over time, the individual students on the programme should be seen to be making real progress in, certainly, the area(s) most clearly identified as the greatest strengths of the individuals concerned. They should be given opportunities to discuss the potential targets that could be devised to guide their work, and define their next steps to real and discernible development. Whether these efforts are resulting in desired outcomes or not, the students should be able to feel the genuine support of the school staff in what they are attempting to achieve.

Too many more able students currently in secondary schools make little real progress once they have been identified. There is insufficient discussion – among the teachers, and between student and teacher – about the subtle, but nevertheless authentic possible areas of growth available to these young people. It is as if the act of identification is itself sufficient. This situation is partly due to the paucity of the QCA level descriptors at this stage; the 'Exceptional performance' criteria for reading, for example, is:

Pupils confidently sustain their responses to a demanding range of texts, developing their ideas and referring in detail to aspects of language, structure and presentation. They make apt and careful comparison between texts, including consideration of audience, purpose and form. They identify and analyse argument, opinion and alternative interpretations, making cross-references where appropriate. (DfEE / QCA 1999)

Which raises more questions about the skills of reading than it answers.

A substantial challenging curriculum

There is good evidence already mentioned to suggest that many students are bored with their English work in the early stages of the secondary school, and those who are most able are often the most bored. I meet and talk with Year 7 students who lead two quite separate literacy/literary lives; one in school and another outside, because what is on offer in classrooms is simply too undemanding or fails to meet their needs. Careful and honest curriculum re-appraisal and review should be undertaken in many English departments with the more able students specifically in mind. Just as most planning that takes place in the classrooms of all subjects begins from considering the needs of the average students, including a few support mechanisms for the least confident, and then – a long way behind – devising something at the level of those of higher ability, so the curriculum is usually designed with same order of priorities.

Rethinking the English curriculum for the learning needs of all students

Teachers of English should try to stand at some distance from the content of their previously accepted curriculum and begin thinking more broadly about the shape and size of the whole package on offer. There is a strong tendency for departments to design their work around individual texts, setting up units of study meant to last for a few weeks – most often half a term – based on that single choice.

The first priority in meeting the needs of the more able should be a re-consideration of the content of the curriculum on much broader themes, involving far more textual overlap. This approach is occasionally partially addressed through greater attention to study of a 'genre', such as 'science fiction', or 'the gothic'. Yet, too often, the extent of study is often limited to very few examples of the genre, and with little sense at the planning stage of what progression might mean in that context. Study *of* the particular genre should not be sufficient, as if it is merely a title to be ticked off to indicate that coverage has been achieved. Study *within* the genre is a much more attractive prospect, suggesting possible separate directions of enquiry and research, some of which are likely to be proposed by the students. In many respects, an effective curriculum for the most able students enables them to reach an independent 'flying-off' point, from which they can launch into unique and personalised directions, probably mostly not anticipated or expected by their teachers.

This curriculum would mean departments being very clear about their 'core' learning priorities, and what might be essential to include within it to ensure that students are then sufficiently prepared for any particular direction they might choose. On the accompanying CD is one such developed curriculum plan I have been attempting to construct. It makes an assumption about a learning programme in English covering five years from Year 7 to Year 11. it does not begin with the standard components of reading, writing, speaking and listening. Another curriculum outline, suggested by the former English Adviser at Becta, Sally Tweddle, before her untimely death, is also included to illustrate that there are different ways of approaching curriculum design.

Further reading

Scholes, Robert (1998) *The Rise and Fall of English.* New Haven & London: Yale University Press.

Goodwyn, Andrew (ed.) (2000) *English in the Digital Age.* London: Cassell.

DfEE (2001) *Key Stage 3 National Strategy – Framework for Teaching English: Years 7, 8 and 9.* London: DfEE.

Providing the Best Learning Environment for More Able Students in English

What this chapter is about

> This chapter outlines and describes some of the features and characteristics of an English department that enable more able learners to make the fullest possible progress, in a context of independent learning.
> Departments will need to be positive about identification, and to determine and establish an ethos that comprises a range of desirable supportive attitudes.

Departmental expectations: looking out for ...

An essential feature of promoting and developing more able students in English is the important belief by their English teachers that there will be a proportion of students in any cohort who qualify for that status in their school. Students will only be properly identified as 'more able' if their teachers are looking out for them, and their needs are fully valued. A few students will quickly impress their teachers about their obvious greater ability, but not all. For reasons explored in previous chapters, students may not want to be identified, or may not even realise that they have the sorts of qualities that would lead them to be perceived in this manner. Schools also have to be prepared to employ wide-ranging criteria in their identification procedures, encompassing a number of varied skills, not limiting themselves to a few traditionally accepted superficial criteria.

Those students who qualify as being 'more able' will differ from school to school. A few independent and grammar schools, because of their rigorous selection entry procedures, might well expect all students in each intake to be above average ability, relative to the rest of the population. English departments in more challenging schools, however, might only have three or four such students in any year group. Whatever the context, the likelihood of establishing the correct circumstances in which more able students will achieve their greatest potential will only come about when the departmental staff are actively looking out for these particular young people and treat them appropriately as a result of that identification. These expectations are still new in some schools.

Ways of supporting more able students in English

It would be glib and easy to state that schools intending to serve their more able students properly should be guided by good policies, as policies of themselves will not bring about the necessary ethos in which the more able will thrive. Positive attitudes and good practices driven by vision and a sense of real challenge are far more likely to contribute to the most effective provision. English departments of their own accord will probably not influence the senior management team of their schools, but the accompanying CD contains an outline policy and a booklet considering more general issues to do with providing properly for more able students, which may help in describing the wider context.

Teachers will need to have a clear view about what sorts of developing qualities they are attempting to bring about in their students. They will need to be really clear about what sorts of accomplishments those students might be able to achieve and ways in which they will be expecting those young people to operate in their studies, given all the most supportive circumstances. Students who are already exceptional readers when arriving in secondary school, for example, should not be neglected or expected to get on with their own devices: they should be regarded as potential learners in reading, with the capacity to make further progress – just like all the other students. Yet there are currently few models of successful departments with a consistent history of establishing the most supportive environment in which more able students can fully flourish. The next section explores possible appropriate scenarios.

Paying attention to the person inside the 'more able' label

Professor George Betts and Jolene Kercher devised the Autonomous Learner Model (ALM; 1981/1999) to promote self-directed learning in gifted and talented students. The major goal of the model is to facilitate the growth of students as independent, self-directed learners, with the development of skills, concepts and positive attitudes within the cognitive, emotional and social domains – in many respects, an early forerunner of the personalisation developments currently occupying educational thought in England.

The model consists of five major dimensions:

1   **orientation** – understanding giftedness, group-building activities, self/personal development;

2   **individual development** – inter/intra personal understanding, learning skills, use of technology, university/career awareness, organisational and productivity skills;

3   **enrichment** – courses, explorations, investigations, cultural activities, community service, excursions, camps;

4   **seminars** – small group presentations of futuristic, problematic, controversial, general interest or advanced knowledge topics;

5   **in-depth study** – individual projects, group projects, mentorships, presentations, assessment of self and others.

The first dimension asserts that able students should have opportunities to discuss what is meant by such terms as 'giftedness' and 'more able' and their perceived abilities. These researchers recognise that educators often pay too much attention to the cognitive issues associated with ability, but not enough to the affective. We need to be equally aware of who these young people are and how they feel and react to procedures and institutions which identify them in this particular way before we start planning for the extra attainment we seek from them.

Knowing who these young people are and what their place in the world might be is an essential prerequisite for developing programmes designed to bring about better learners. This is an area of knowledge about students really necessary for effective monitoring. Attention to the 'student voice' in the mentoring context should make it possible to align learners more positively with the learning programmes their teachers are establishing.

Transition

The best start more able students can enjoy in secondary schools will be in circumstances where effective transition arrangements between the primary school and receiving school are firmly in place. The secondary school staff will already have received accurate information about the incoming able students, and possibly seen evidence of their enhanced ability or heard about their particular achievements. The students will not waste time in the first few weeks of their secondary career having to prove to their new teachers just what it is they are capable of doing, but will participate in planned exercises and activities that readily encourage demonstration of the talents they possess. They will not waste time, either, in low-level events, which offer little or no challenge.

If able students can be given an opportunity to talk to a member of the English staff, or other appropriate adult, quite early in their secondary career, so much the better. They might explore possible targets they wish to achieve, or share personal interests and pastimes they would want to pursue through their coming studies. As a result of this preliminary, reassuring conversation, able students should feel comfortable in their new setting very quickly and energised to work as successfully as they can.

Projecting towards what more able students might become

Each more able student is unique. Every more able student is different from every other more able student: there is no definitive mould into which they can be poured, leading to the same educational and personal outcomes.

The subject 'English' is also very broad in its spread, and covers many areas of language-based experience. It is not at all helpful, therefore, merely to propose as a target that a student 'improves in English', as that would be too vague and unfocused an analysis. It is necessary to be far more specific about any potential areas in which intended progression will be calculated to occur.

This demanding requirement makes the task of projecting ahead for each student difficult for English teachers – but by no means impossible. Good identification procedures are the first important consideration for teachers in establishing the essential needs of already impressive students. If the student is an acute and perceptive analytical reader, then a projection to do with developing those reading skills even further must be a proper starting point. Another student might display sophisticated creative writing skills, in which case the supporting teachers will be considering carefully which details of such skills could constitute further proper development. Students themselves need to become focused and acute target-setters, relative to their own developing understanding about themselves as learners.

Independent learning

In the twenty-first century, professional educators are beginning to recognise that many of the ways the educational system operated in the past have been too blunt and mechanised. The school system was based on the factory system, which was the predominant model of organising the through-put of the largest possible number of products in the shortest time in the Victorian age. A result of this approach was the neglect of *independent learning*. Few students have ever enjoyed the opportunity in most schools to develop work or projects in ways that hugely suit the learner. How students might achieve that very desirable skill has, also, rarely been outlined in detail.

Independent learners

- choose study projects that grow from their interests, but extend their horizons and their knowledge and challenge previous assumptions within clear learning outlines;

- proceed in their studies without constant supervision;

- can work in environments they choose, most beneficial to enhancing their studies;

- seek help when they really have exhausted a large range of other possibilities;

- can see learning and study as holistic exercises, with a clear overview of how their studies contribute to broader understanding;

- are enthusiastic about their work and self-motivated;

- can use a range of learning techniques and resources;

- set themselves important and searching questions;

- are very goal-orientated;

- work with others when they see benefits in collaboration;

- set themselves and meet challenging but realistic deadlines.

Few of these ways of working are currently the normal *modus operandi* for most secondary students in English classrooms, but they should be vital components of a sophisticated agenda for the future. The generic contexts listed above would be worth working towards as a shared departmental enterprise, with the aim of establishing expectations in which individual students could then pursue a huge range of possible study units. There is no reason why students should not participate in study units alongside their peers, while at the same time negotiating the setting-off points for further, individualised study where those opportunities are offered.

This projection should not be regarded as a distant, pie-in-the-sky, woolly aspiration. Bringing about a culture that allows independent learners to flourish should not be too difficult to establish in current departmental practice, certainly with those students in KS3 and in post-16 study not immediately facing the prospect of external examination. Some teachers might well protest about the constraining prescriptiveness of the English curriculum, but such departments are probably not yet much practised in exploring the flexible alternatives in English studies that have been encouraged recently. The criteria for independent learning set out above will certainly be a fundamental requirement for any department wishing to offer a genuinely personalised educational experience, which all schools are being urged to consider as a next step forward in their development planning.

Bringing about independent learning

English departments will need to consider the following kinds of approach.

Increasing the level of student choice of study

Currently most departments dictate to their students both the titles and sorts of texts they will be studying, and the manner of that study. The reasons for these choices are often not to do with student learning, but depend on resources the department already possesses, and practices that have become accepted and usual over time. While much of the study in English takes place around matters of content rather than around defined learning positions, the situation described above is likely to persist. If, however, a number of ongoing 'strands of learning' were to be agreed by the English department, that covered all five years of secondary education, the resources through which those 'strands' might be realised would become subordinate to the actual learning that might be pursued through their use. So, for instance, 'narrative' might be the name of one such 'strand' through which students would be expected to make progress from Year 7 to Year 11. Their possible areas of study could then be conducted through different groupings of texts in different media, such as: film; computer games; graphic novels and comics, as well as the more traditional literary book. Students might wish to explore 'narrative' in drama, or through different poetic forms. It would be possible – although in organisational terms, not very feasible – for a whole class to be studying and making real progress in their understanding of 'narrative', but with every member of the class working with a unique configuration of texts. A more likely situation could involve groups of reasonably like-minded students working with a shared collection of relevant resources, agreed by all the group participants.

Starting from student-centred beginning points

Teachers will need to be very aware of the interests and passions of their students, by paying close attention through properly focused 'student voice' exercises. Students who have been effectively empowered to make good choices will benefit from this degree of independence, which makes valuable preparation for the secondary school experience really vital. Teachers might have to be prepared to receive ideas or suggestions about projects from their students about which they themselves have little knowledge or expertise.

This degree of knowledge about individual students is a more generous definition of 'assessment for learning', considered in greater detail in Chapter 5 (Personalisation). What might also require greater importance, however, in this context would be very effective *transition arrangements*.

Preparing for and properly supporting study that will not necessarily take place in the classroom

Teachers must be prepared to expect that their students might not necessarily have to be present in the classroom to be working effectively. Indeed, some may not even be in the school. Good initial supervisory skills will be required to ensure that the study 'units' are properly understood by all parties and carefully established, that they work to sensible but challenging deadlines, and that 'monitoring' arrangements are securely in place to make sure that the projects stay 'on course' and are having the desired effects on the learners. From those beginning circumstances it should be possible to arrange times when students meet their tutors or when their teachers might access their current activities through shared 'learning platforms' the school will have set up for such shared interactions.

Learning platforms

Learning platforms are developing areas of computer technology being trialled in increasingly large numbers of classrooms. Students are allocated a unique space on the internet, called a 'learning platform', that can be accessed only by themselves and their teachers. The space, or 'platform', is capable of storing all the information and references the learner acquires, including still and moving images and sound texts. Teachers can 'open' the platform at any time, to check on progress or assess completed work, and students can study wherever they wish. This technology is one of the most significant ways in which young people will be able to pursue personalised programmes in the future.

Adjusting the power and responsibility structures in classrooms

Most of the study that takes place nationally in the majority of classrooms is determined by teachers, organising what their students will undertake for results that, often, have little to do with the real interests or skills of the learner. Researchers, like myself, visiting classrooms asking students what, or who, they are working for, regularly hear them respond, 'my teacher'. Only a minority of students actually fully realise that they are, in fact, studying for their own benefit. It would take a huge shift in the entire education culture for all students to acknowledge and accept genuine responsibility for their own progress and success, but it is a thoroughly worthwhile goal that must be pursued.

It will be absolutely essential that such a change is gradually brought about in the next decade. Teachers might, in that process, consider in detail the implications of moving from their current position of 'instructor' to one of 'lead learner' or 'coach', modelling the processes of effective learning for their students to emulate. Indeed, this is a particularly appropriate time for teachers to set off on learning pathways that are new to themselves, with so many changes in areas like technology and curriculum intruding strongly. Young people will need to place themselves very firmly at the centre of their learning processes and be prepared to negotiate carefully the directions of study they wish to pursue, and what potential likely benefits will be derived from those decisions.

Coaching students in the skills of putting and exploring probing and searching questions

Most students do not, at present, arrive at secondary school with strongly developed questioning skills. Even able students rarely enjoy the opportunity to put good questions, even if the opportunities arise. They will need practice in those fundamental approaches, if they are to engage successfully with their work through better enquiry.

Recently, many schools, as part of the promotion of 'thinking skills', have encouraged or made time for the understanding of 'higher order' thinking, which involves, among other developments, the improving of questioning abilities.

Robin Alexander and his colleagues at the Department of Education at the University of Cambridge are working on developing programmes of 'dialogic' learning, based on successful models of questioning and subsequent talk seen to work effectively in countries such as Russia. These processes require students to be prepared and confident about standing at the front of the class, or any other prominent position, raising matters of detail about their work, or explaining how they are processing the matter with which they are engaged. The findings from most surveys ever conducted into the use of talk in classrooms indicate that an overwhelming proportion of the available time is taken up by teachers, with a fraction allocated to the learners. Much of what little time students do occupy is then given over to answering closed questions, usually on topics that the teacher already knows about. Students are not practised in challenging themselves, their peers or their teachers, yet more able students will be expected to take these vital skills to their university courses if they are to succeed at the appropriate level.

Peter Thomas, a hugely experienced teacher, researcher and academic in respect of more able English students, has written in *The Secondary English Magazine* (Thomas 2007) about establishing supportive questioning techniques in secondary English lessons, based on the principles of Benjamin Bloom and his colleagues (Bloom 1956). Bloom proposed a 'taxonomy of learning' in which there are six levels, moving through the lowest order processes to the highest: knowledge – comprehension – application – analysis – synthesis – evaluation.

Different kinds of questions arise at the various levels of the taxonomy, such as:

- 'Just asking' – for checking matters of information (knowledge):

    Is it true that ...?

    Do you agree that ...?

    Are you one of those who thinks ...?

- 'Asking for application' – (application):

    Do you think there is anything you can do ...?

    What would you do if ...?

    Is there any point in trying to convince those who think that ...?

- 'Asking for analysis/qualification' (analysis):

    Is it *always* true that ...?

    Would you *sometimes* agree/not agree that ...?

Would you worry if ...?

- 'Asking to synthesise/hypothesise' (synthesis):

When would you expect ...?

What would happen if ...?

How would this change ...?

- 'Asking for moral evaluation' (evaluation):

Should we be ashamed that ...?

Why are we able to ...?

Who is to blame for ...?

 A more detailed example of using Bloom's taxonomy in respect of English is included on the accompanying CD.

Providing a range of technologies and training in using those technologies

Students will need access to as much digital technology as they can get their hands on, in a changing educational world where technologies are likely to grow exponentially and be ascribed increasing importance in the next two decades. Some students will continue to conduct a large proportion of their studies with book texts, although the 'technology of the book' is itself due for change in the very near future. Others will want to conduct internet research, and even study emerging texts brought about as a result of the internet, e.g. blogs. Some may want to employ technology capable of viewing film and moving-image, and making and editing, and re-editing already published moving-image texts. Yet others may want to explore and create language through audio technologies, or a mixture of audio and pictorial. Whatever technologies students require, schools will have to try to ensure that their learners are not disadvantaged by problems of lack of access, or the lack of knowledge of their teachers.

As in all other respects, any provision made for the more able students should not be regarded as exclusive to that group. What is good for more able students must also be equally worthwhile for their peers. It should be clear from the conditions set out above, however, that more able students, fully involved in their studies, should have the wherewithal to experience massive benefits from the climate described. They should be capable of already raising more challenging questions before arriving in such an environment and will probably have a more developed repertoire of English-related experiences from which to choose their own projects rather more independently. More able students, by their very definition, are also more likely to be able to make links between ideas, and bring together texts and technologies in more impressive ways than their more average peers.

Student groupings and differentiation

As education in English moved towards mixed ability grouping in the 1970s and 80s, so began a heated discussion about the most supportive grouping arrangements in which more able students would flourish best. It was, and still is, a common perception that more able students are penalised and cannot achieve as well if they have to study alongside less able peers, but continuing research has suggested that the issue is really more complex than merely educating more able pupils in special groups. Dr Susan Hallam, of the Institute of Education in London, claims that what is really important in English is the quality of teaching and whether pupils have access to the full curriculum, not the constitution of the class at all. A summary of her work (accesssible online at http://ioewebserver.ioe.ac.uk/ioe/cms/get.asp?cid=1397&1397_1=5370) concludes that there is no evidence that ability grouping automatically raises standards. Her research, however, also shows that mixed ability classes in which teachers teach at whole-class level to an 'imaginary average child' are not the answer. Brighter children are bored because they are not stretched, and lower ability children find it hard to keep up. Slavin (1990) reviewed 29 studies, using a method of best synthesis, and concluded that the effect of ability grouping on academic attainment was limited.

There is never a solidly correct answer to this sort of issue, but one of the best sorts of provision would seem to be the setting up of groups of students with similar attainment within the class, in the manner also recommended by Professor Carol Tomlinson, an important expert in differentiation at the University of Virginia. Tomlinson sets out a number of conditions that lead to more successful differentiation, more sophisticated than the simple versions of the tiers 'must', 'should' and 'could' which are the stuff of much current lesson planning. Professor Tomlinson (1993) outlines the concept of 'differentiation', which she claims should be 'concept focused and principle driven', as follows:

- articulated philosophy of student differences;

- planned assessment and compacting;

- variable pacing;

- planned variation in content;

- flexible classroom arrangements;

- planned variation in how students demonstrate their understanding of what they have learned;

- planned variations in students' products;

- consistent use of flexible groups;

- individual goal setting, assessment, and grading;

- mentoring;

- grading on individual growth and progress.

Worth noticing is Professor Tomlinson's insistence on 'planned' matters and outcomes, rather than results that merely emerge, which used to be what happened quite often in an arrangement called 'differentiation by outcome'.

Recognising that students of different abilities can be successfully educated together in the same room, as long as the central shared learning is substantial, fully understood by all and approached from appropriate starting points, is the most effective structuring for all learners. What teachers can do, however, is to ensure that students, of whatever ability, take part in enterprises which establish the following pathways of learning:

1   **Concrete to abstract.** Learners advanced in a subject often benefit from tasks that involve more abstract materials, representations, ideas, or applications than less advanced peers.

2   **Simple to complex.** Learners advanced in a subject often benefit from tasks that are more complex in resources, research, issues, problems, skills, or goals than less advanced peers.

3   **Basic to transformational.** Learners advanced in a subject often benefit from tasks that require greater transformation or manipulation of information, ideas, materials, or applications than less advanced peers.

4   **Fewer facets to multi-facets.** Learners advanced in a subject often benefit from tasks that have more facets or parts in their directions, connections within or across subjects, or planning and execution than less advanced peers.

5   **Smaller leaps to greater leaps.** Learners advanced in a subject often benefit from tasks that require greater mental leaps in insight, application, or transfer than less advanced peers.

6   **More structured to more open.** Learners advanced in a subject often benefit from tasks that are more open in regard to solutions, decisions, and approaches than less advanced peers.

7   **Less independence to greater independence.** Learners advanced in a subject often benefit from greater independence in planning, designing, and self-monitoring than less advanced peers.

8   **Quicker to slower.** Learners advanced in a subject will sometimes benefit from rapid movement through prescribed materials and tasks. At other times, they may require a greater amount of time with a given study than less advanced peers so that they may explore the topic in greater depth and/or breadth.

In differentiating the curriculum, Tomlinson says, teachers are not dispensers of knowledge but organisers of learning opportunities. To provide optimal learning opportunities the classroom environment must be changed to accommodate the interests and abilities of the learner.

Joseph Renzulli, in his paper 'Five dimensions of differentiation' (1997), identifies similar aspects of differentiation to those described above, while defining goals that each dimension should include for a truly differentiated approach. Goals related to the five dimensions are:

1   **content** – enrich the curriculum through focusing on curriculum concepts and structuring knowledge excitingly;

2   **process** – use a variety of teaching techniques and materials to enhance and motivate a range of learning styles in the students;

3   **product** – improve students' cognitive development and ability to express themselves;

4   **classroom** – enhance students' learning comfort by changing groupings and the physical area of the environment;

5   **teacher** – the teacher plays an important part in encouraging learning by sharing personal knowledge of topics related to the curriculum as well as being sensitive to the learner's personal interests, collections, hobbies, and enthusiasm about issues surrounding content area.

Extra-curricular activities

While the really important learning and progress should occur as a result of an appropriate and well-directed mainstream curriculum, schools can also assist more able students to grow and feel challenged in activities outside normal school class time. There could be many opportunities for able students to continue to make progress other than in formally assessed situations.

Clubs and societies are the first obvious arena in which more able students in English might find possibilities of employing their skills in different and exciting ways. So some might study and make films; some might write and perform plays; some might debate; some might write; and others might share reading situations in the manner of modern book clubs, all under the supervision of enthusiastic teachers, or occasionally directed by the young people themselves. All these instances would usually be on the school premises. Sometimes, other agencies may offer further study and intellectual ventures. Mary Kellett, a teacher at the Open University, for instance, offers sessions for able children as researchers, dealing with hugely sophisticated projects, in after-school times. Other 'master class' situations are regularly organised in many different areas, and more able students will often appreciate being directed towards them.

Students should be introduced to the 'Young, Gifted and Talented' website – ygt. dcsf.gov.uk/ – where they will find a dveloping 'virtual academy', offering courses and events. There is also a closed chatline for contact with others sharing the same interests. Writers' workshops and youth theatre projects are alternative activities to which more able English students could be directed, to gain insights and skills simply not possible to acquire in the very busy school curriculum.

Developing the role of parents and carers

The most effective provision for more able students of English will occur in circumstances where the school values the role parents can play in a vital triangle: learner–school–parents. At the simplest level, students will spend far more time with their families than they will at school. Apprising parents and carers about what the school is trying to achieve with their children has to be a necessary link in the chain of communications. Some schools are very coy about sharing information about their able students with parents, even to the extent of not informing them that identification has taken place. This is a very questionable situation. Virtually all parents are aware of their children's abilities, and are delighted to assist in any manageable practical manner.

They could be encouraged to ensure that students work to their full potential at home, are guided to wards certain activities and pastimes that enhance educational performance, and help by providing resources and other access to materials and devices for extending already developed interests. Knowing about the intellectual prowess of their children, can also allow parents to talk in suitable terms to their children about plans for their future and the relationship between the young learners and their various targets and aspirations.

Further reading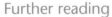

Betts, G.T. and Knapp, J. (1981) 'The autonomous learner model: a secondary model'. In *Secondary Programs for the Gifted and Talented*, ed. A. Arnold. Los Angeles, CA: National/State Leadership Training Institute for the Gifted and Talented.

Hallam, S. (2002) *Ability Grouping in Schools*. London: Institute of Education.

Learning in English

What this chapter is about

> The movement from teaching to learning
> Some difficulties to do with establishing effective learning in the past
> Building a curriculum for the future
> Describing effective learning in English
> What long-term, medium-term and short-term planning could look like
> Models for planning for learning

The shift towards learning and the difficulties of learning in English

The major discernible shift in education in English schools since the beginning of the twenty-first century has been the movement towards effective *learning*. Only a decade previously the emphasis had been firmly on *teaching*, but a number of significant publications, such as *Inside the Black Box: Raising Standards through Classroom Assessment* by Dylan Wiliam and Paul Black (1998), and a continuing re-appraisal of the core purposes of schools have brought about a fundamental change in priorities. Wiliam and Black argued the clearest possible case, from the evidence of their research, for understanding that students learned much more when they were fully aware of what they were supposed to be learning, and when those intentions had been clearly articulated *for* them, and subsequently *by* them, in a language they completely understood:

> Whilst hardly counting as a scientific study, a quick survey of the titles of books and publications concerned with this subject during the last 30 years would soon reveal that much less has been written about the learning expected in English classrooms than is devoted to the teaching which has taken place. (Dean 2004: 1)

So, senior managers in many schools now recognise that guiding students towards understanding what they should be *learning* is the most effective way of engaging those young people with their studies, leading, in turn, to higher standards. 'Learning how to learn' has become the focus of much recent professional development, and is regarded as a vital component of the 'personalised' programmes being devised across the country. Researchers such as Shirley Clarke and Guy Claxton have helped teachers refashion the focus of planning towards much sharper learning outcomes.

The difficulties of defining learning in English

This shift in emphasis towards learning, however, has not always been easy for English teachers. Planning in the subject has not traditionally addressed learning, although it has often been about developing the many skills required for reading, writing, speaking and listening. Yet the major historical tendency has been to devise activities around texts, through which students were expected to gain a number of broad insights, leading – it is hoped – to more effective meaning-making with other, unfamiliar texts subsequently encountered. Considerable energy has also been expended on assisting students to make personal responses to their study texts. Requiring English teachers to make their learning more specific has led to a number of problems and tensions in some departments, causing a number of important questions to be raised in a number of schools about the nature of the subject itself.

A well-established bias of English in recent times has been towards development of the affective elements in students: a model of the subject depicted as one of 'personal growth' by Professor Brian Cox and his committee in 1988, when charged with creating the original English curriculum (Cox 1991). Research by Andy Goodwyn and Kate Findlay at Reading University confirmed that a significant majority of Heads of English continued to espouse this as their priority view of English almost a decade after the introduction of that curriculum. Such an approach is difficult to articulate in terms of learning, beyond developing students' personal responses and feelings. The introduction by the government of the Key Stage 3 Strategy (subsequently the Secondary Strategy) in 2001 has encouraged a shift in the subject towards a greater emphasis on language, but the Strategy documentation has not promoted or modelled effective learning approaches (Dean 2004).

Thus, it has become evident that there is a major difficulty in English to do with whether learning should be about acquiring skills or developing an 'appreciation' of texts in a much wider manner. The introduction of the English secondary strategy in the early part of the twenty-first century disturbed a number of departments. They became concerned that they were being expected to concentrate on 'literacy' at the expense of the 'literature' which had meant so much to the majority of English teachers (Goodwyn 2004). These nice distinctions should not distract teachers constructing worthwhile learning programmes for more able students. They should be developing schemes of work, capable of establishing good insights into an ever increasing background of textual proliferation, including an understanding of the necessary skills, across a range of texts, to access and demonstrate the biggest possible repertoire of meaning-making abilities.

Alternative English Curriculum Model: a text framework

I/we	represent	something	through somebody's offices	by some means	for my/our reasons	for someone
Originator	**Representational medium**	**Modes of transmission**	**Gatekeeper**	**Form**	**Purpose**	**Audience**
single	multimedia	**electronic/digital:** DVD, email, phone, TV, games box, video		**stable and/to plastic:** liturgy or memo/email chat, scripted drama/improvisation, book/word-processed file	**self-generated to multiple-generated:** chosen to, prescribed	**remote/close:** culturally, geographically, socially, linguistically, temporally
	language: speech/writing	**print:** printout, book, magazine, newspaper	**individual/institutional:** teacher, editor, conference, controller, publisher, ISP, Board of Censors, web-nanny		persuade	
	iconographic: photograph/computer-generated graphics	handwriting		**linear and/to non-linear:** novel, encyclopaedia, computer conference/hypertext	explore	**single/multiple:** class of peers/range of schools
	sound	spoken	**visible/invisible:** line manager, internet provider		inform	
multiple: pair, committee, working group, editorial, multi-national communications group, publisher	**performance:** drama, role-play	**combination:** video conference with data transfer		**size:** newspaper article, War and Peace, hypertext card/ CD-Rom	entertain	individual/group
					express	
by someone	which is represented	something	through somebody's offices	by some means	for my/our reasons	I/we read/view

English for Gifted and Talented Students. SAGE © Geoff Dean 2008

Some of the uncertainty of what to include in a mature English scheme of work has been brought about as a result of the traditional practice of studying single texts, which has become the *modus operandi* of most programmes. So, a Year 9 class might read and look closely into *Macbeth*. The learning intentions of a typical lesson in these circumstances could be

> to know what takes place in Act 2, scene iii of *Macbeth*,

suggesting not only a very plodding approach to the play but also missing the point entirely about the sorts of literary learning the study of *Macbeth* could properly be intended to address. English teachers will, with some justification, claim that the distorting power of the Key Stage 3 SAT has been responsible for such an approach, but this model of study is not only restricted to the study of Shakespeare plays. In Key Stage 4, as has been discussed elsewhere, the curriculum content of most English departments comprises little more than a study of the texts to be examined at GCSE. Therefore, the learning range for that age group does not often extend much further than a limited focus on those texts. More able students, more than any others, are not likely to thrive or make much personal progress in such limited circumstances.

John West-Burnham, a respected educational academic and researcher, regularly emphasises the value of 'deep learning'. He defines 'deep learning' as that learning which profoundly changes the learner, the learner's perspective on the world and significantly repositions the learner relative to future learning. It is also the sort of learning which stays with the learner, unlike the transience of 'shallow learning', and can be recalled with the minimum of stimulation at necessary moments in the future. It has weight and value. It is the sort of learning we should be establishing for all learners, but the more able should be encountering it regularly.

Advisers and inspectors visiting English classrooms often see how 'learning' is not properly understood or firmly established in many lessons in the subject. It is not unusual to see virtually the same lessons in poetry, for instance, taking place in years 7, 9 and 10. The learning in most of these contexts is shallow, directed towards a single poem, or a very limited range of poems, and insufficiently affects the learners because the intended learning was not substantial enough to make real impact. Students are not being encouraged to engage robustly with the 'matter' of poetry in general and they fail to have a strongly shaped understanding of what poets are attempting to convey through that medium. When students are re-introduced to poetry two or three years later, they often have to retrace the same ground, making very little, if any, progress. All students would benefit from a curriculum programme which considered carefully the stages of learning in poetry, and ensured that each time those students returned to the topic they would continue to move forward academically and in their readiness to make more mature personal responses. More able students would flourish where that sort of emphasis was made.

Good readers

Good readers

- see images

- hear a reading voice

- predict what will happen

- speculate

- ask questions, tease at puzzles

- pass comment

- feel

- empathise

- rationalise what is happening

- re-read

- reinterpret

- relate to patterns

- relate to own experience

- pass judgements – likes, dislikes

- relate to previous reading experience

- establish a relationship with the narrator

Or make relationships in the following manner

Intertextual relationships

Perfect worlds –

such as that of the Eloi in
The Time Machine, H. G. Wells;
Brave New World, Aldous Huxley

Carefully regulated worlds –

Nineteen Eighty-Four, George Orwell
Waterbound, Jane Stemp

Exodus
Julie Bertagna

Dystopias – new worlds rising where
the old world crumbled:

Mortal Engines, Philip Reeve
The Wind Singer, William Nicholson

Qualities and characteristics of the reader

1   A reader knows that reading is a complex, intellectual endeavour, requiring the reader to draw on a range of active meaning-making skills

    Mentally preparing for any sort of reading

2   A reader deploys previous knowledge of other texts to enable the effective meaning-making of the text being read.

    Knowing all texts relate intertextually

3   A reader is aware that texts are constructed for particular purposes, for identifiable audiences and within recognisable text-types and/or genres.

    Knowing what sort of text it is – and who for

4   A reader can predict the ways texts are likely to work, and uses reading to confirm or readjust those predictions, depending on how typically a text unfolds.

    Predicting/knowing the way texts work

5   A reader is critically active before becoming involved in the substantial body of any text.

    Preparing for a new text by using all available clues

6   A reader is increasingly able to activate a repertoire of critical questions in engagements with new and unfamiliar texts.

    Getting better at asking more about texts

7   A reader knows how to interact appropriately with a variety of text-types and/or genres for particular purposes.

    Knowing that we read differently for different purposes

8   A reader is aware that an important way of demonstrating reading progression is through raising more complex questions about the same text.

    Getting better at asking questions on re-reading

9   A reader is aware that learning to read is a lifelong process.

    Learning to read NEVER stops

10   A reader is aware that other readers do not always read and make meanings in the same ways.

    Knowing we make our own unique meanings

11   A reader can explain why a text might not satisfy the task to which it has been put, or has been rejected, unfinished.

    Knowing how to choose

12   A reader knows that reading improves through monitoring and reflection on own ability and progress.

    Thinking about and re-flecting on reading

What our students will need to make a real success of their futures

A clear view of the future

For too long the English education system has limped along with a totally unsuitable curriculum. Extraordinarily, the system did not acquire a universal guiding curriculum until the late 1980s. Unfortunately, the one it got was almost wholly retrospective and designed to serve a populace living in the concluding years of the industrial revolution (then almost finished), rather than one designed to educate a people preparing for the information revolution (then and now, almost never fully appreciated and, as yet, not wholly welcomed). Even as this book is being written, the Qualifications and Curriculum Agency (QCA), the agency charged with providing and monitoring the English schools' curriculum, is amending the English programme expected to be taught in all classrooms. Yet even this new programme is badly wanting in respect of modern developments, and major problems about not engaging with the real needs of learners in the twenty-first century still remain.

The first of these problems has to do with the failure by schools to articulate the essential sorts of qualities or characteristics thought to be necessary for survival, success, economic well-being, relationship-making and good citizenship in the middle and later parts of the twenty-first century. Having discussed this matter in a number of forums with teachers of different age groups, and business and parental groups, the following list represents a wide consensus regarding the ideally desirable characteristics of a successful learner:

- initiative;

- flexibility and adaptability;

- self-directed;

- an independent learner;

- a practised and regular thinker, always curious;

- a confident communicator – in a range of media;

- a confident user of technology;

- creative and problem-solving;

- responsible for own progress;

- a team player;

- broadly literate across a range of literacies;

- emotionally aware and self-evaluative;

- physically fit and living healthily.

Most of these attributes, which the Gilbert Review (2006) terms 'the soft curriculum', are not currently the real priorities of most secondary schools. Where they are practised and developed, it is usually more by chance rather than by premeditated design. These requirements have to become far more pivotal if the school system is to serve our student body in properly effective ways. Not engaging with these issues actively disadvantages more able students, who need space to develop much broader skills beyond the basic requirements of the standard curriculum. We have to take proper account of the real and fundamental needs of our students, and build them centrally into the secondary curriculum.

Technological and communications growth

> Everyone agrees: the school of the future will be radically different from the model of the last 130 years. Technology will ensure that. (Bennett 2001)

Technology will impact on our future lives in ways most of us still find hard to imagine. Children born since the early 1990s, who take the presence of digital technologies completely for granted, already have a markedly different approach to digital technology compared to the attitudes of their parents. They accept and expect absolutely that computers, mobile telephones and developing tools such as the iPod are a natural part of any communications landscape. They have a mindset shaped and fashioned in a very different world than even their parents, and almost certainly the majority of their teachers, experienced:

> Our young people generally have a much better idea of what the future is bringing than we do. They're already busy adopting new systems for communicating (instant messaging), sharing (blogs), buying and selling (eBay), exchanging (peer-to-peer technology), creating (Flash), meeting (3D worlds), collecting (downloads), coordinating (wikis), evaluating (reputation systems), searching (Google), analyzing (SETI), reporting (camera phones), programming (modding), socializing (chat rooms), and even learning (Web surfing). (Prensky 2006)

All these developments have already significantly changed our ways of communicating in a period of just over a decade since the mid-1990s. Those who work and research in digital technological fields confidently predict that the changes and developments in the next decade will be exponentially greater than anything we have so far experienced. Digital telephony alone will continue to make huge leaps, so that it will be commonplace to see the caller on the screen, as well as being able to watch television, films and other moving text. We have already witnessed in very recent history how the reporting of news events and important matters of personal privacy is being challenged by developments such as the digital video camera incorporated in the mobile phone. The mobile phone itself, which has already developed into a much more sophisticated instrument in the relatively short space of time since its invention, is due to undergo even more startling developments.

A large number of more able students arrive in secondary school with techno-logical skills and capabilities far superior to those of most of their teachers. They have a greater confidence in their own abilities and a much wider knowledge of the actual capacities and potential of various areas of technology than even the ICT staff of many schools. The phenomenal increase in the use of telephones and the expanding facility of texting has been accompanied by a completely changed, pared-down written language that alarms the linguistic purists. Similarly the incor-poration of the video camera into the mobile telephone and the steady decrease in prices of advanced digital video cameras have enabled virtually anybody to become a film-maker. Every new computer with an operating system of Windows XP or later will, by default, contain a most accessible editing facility called Movie Maker. Apple Macs have similar programs. Websites such as YouTube offer a forum for these texts to be broadcast to potential audiences of millions.

Yet the National Curriculum for English in Key Stage 3, currently being reviewed once again, still fails to acknowledge the immense role technology plays in young people's lives at this time, and is utterly blinkered about its likely effects in the future. Despite this lamentable shortcoming, English teachers who are serving their more able students in any effective way will need to keep abreast of develop-ments, to encourage their learners to incorporate into the classroom new devices as they become widely available, and to be aware of the new kinds of outcome that such technology will create for wider understanding and exploration of even further potential in English studies.

Less content and greater curriculum flexibility

A Victorian educationalist would have little trouble recognising the school cur-riculum in the first decade of the twenty-first century, as it resembles that of 1890 in virtually every respect. The learning experiences in nearly all secondary schools are organised around hour blocks of separate subjects, usually put together in sequences which serve the interests of the teaching staff and the institution, not those of the learners. There is little planning for overlap of work or learning be-tween separate subjects, and even within the subject areas there is little opportu-nity to tap into the actual interests of the participating students.

The content expected to be shared with students in the English programme has often caused real problems and much dispute over time, particularly as the subject 'English' is such a highly politicised area. When the first National Curriculum was introduced in the late 1980s, the English content reflected the kind of curriculum from public schools of the 1940s and 1950s that would have been thoroughly familiar to the government ministers and civil servants who attended them. A canon of 'classical' texts formed the core, with virtually no reference to modern writers, poets and playwrights. A study anthology of literature, supposedly designed for students in Year 9, actually included a passage from Dr Johnson's *Rasselas*, a work of deeply sonorous pessimism, wholly inappropriate for the majority of 14-year-olds. Graham Frater, a former staff inspector HMI for English, was moved to write passionately:

> A conspiracy theorist could be forgiven for imagining that SEAC [the forerunner of QCA] was seeking to make literature unappealing for fourteen-year-olds, perhaps in the hope of tempting more of them into A-level Physics later on. There is almost total exclusion of those areas of life most likely to resonate with the adolescent reader, such as young love, generational conflict, or the tensions between self and society. There is little of what makes literature powerful, or which challenges received views, little tension, conflict or drama. (Frater 1993)

Some of those early strictures have subsequently been ameliorated, but the current English curriculum still expects the study of 'pre-1914' textual material, as if that date somehow embodies magical transformative qualities, and passages of a prescribed Shakespeare play (on which a national assessment of general reading ability is conducted for 14-year-old students). I do not wish to convey a misleading impression here. I fully endorse the right of all, and certainly more able, students to read and study texts written in former times – indeed, I believe that a programme without them would be wholly insubstantial – but not in the contexts currently demanded. It would be extremely difficult for a visionary English department to put together a really motivating, wide-ranging textual programme, that would suit the needs and interests of all its students, in the prevailing circumstances.

All students should, of course, enjoy an entitlement to a full curriculum. Before the National Curriculum was introduced the English programme in many departments was not very broadly developed and large areas of the subject could be and were neglected in many schools. Yet, for more able students, it should be possible for departments to weave students' own interests and preoccupations into an absorbing and motivating project, still satisfying any legal entitlement. If independent learning and personalisation (see Chapter 5) are to prevail as ways of study in the future, these essential adjustments will have to be made to the system.

Uninventing testing

Students in English schools are the most heavily tested in the world. But for our more able students the testing regime means very little and serves virtually no useful purpose. Teachers do not require a test to confirm what they already clearly know about the attainment of their most able students; the evidence is glaringly obvious every time they meet with them.

A student capable of achieving a Level 7 during Key Stage 3 would certainly be regarded as more able by any right-thinking English department. Yet the criterion which has existed until very recently for adjudging a student at Level 7 in reading is really too bland to be of much help in shaping the appropriate programme to enable that student to flourish:

> Pupils show understanding of the ways in which meaning and information are conveyed in a range of texts. They articulate personal and critical responses to poems, plays and novels, showing awareness of their thematic, structural and linguistic features. They select and synthesise a range of information from a variety of sources. (DfE/QCA 1999: 3)

Assessment of able readers

These suggestions for assessment come from a Reading Project conducted in Milton Keynes to explore how to make already able readers even more successful

While it was generally agreed that the assessment should always be rigorous and worthwhile, it was also understood that the processes of written outcomes and/or comprehension-based assessment would not be sufficiently suitable for judging the development of more able readers. Other criteria were, therefore, sought.

Agreement was reached about tracing development through some or all of the following areas:

1	Persistence	Pupils are determined to continue reading, and understand and articulate good reasons for improving.
2	Genre knowledge and experience	Pupils to be encouraged to read from a wide range of genres, and to be familiar with the many available genre types.
3	From the literal to the inferential	Tracing the ability of pupils to recognise that language represents ideas and interpretations beyond the obvious and superficial – that texts can be 'about' ideas, etc.
4	'Me as a reader'	Using the GD proforma (see 'Concept Map of the Reader' on this CD), or similar devices, to interview pupils on a regular basis as a means of tracking reading developments across a range of reading strategies.
5	Increasing fluency and intonation of reading aloud from prose, poetry and play script texts	Supporting and developing readers to convince and engage an audience fully when reading aloud unfamiliar texts.
6	Intertextual knowledge	Readers' developing understanding of the 'communities of texts' – recognising the same plot or sort of character represented in a novel, or a film or comic, for instance, reading more than one text by the same author.
7	Increasing independence as a chooser and reader of texts	Tracking the ability of pupils to explain what they might be wanting to read next, and why – and whether their choices turned out to be successes or not.
8	Increasing reading range	Deliberately selecting texts outside normal areas of choice as personal challenges.
9	Recommenders and/or presenters	Improving the ways that pupils offer their peers suggestions and recommendations about texts they have enjoyed, and would wish others to try.
10	Raising questions about the text	Pupils' own growing skills of digging more deeply into the matter and issues of a text.
11	Developing self-evaluation strategies and approaches	Pupils' abilities to explain and articulate their feelings and perceptions of themselves as readers – and the ability to explore those reactions with increasing depth and breadth of response.

Even the updated version of this criterion, suggested on the QCA website in February 2007, still fails to excite English departments to devise areas of study likely to stimulate greater engagement of a positive kind:

> Pupils show understanding of the ways in which meaning and information are conveyed in a range of texts. They articulate personal and critical responses to poems, plays and novels, showing awareness of their thematic, structural and linguistic features. *They understand why some texts have been particularly valued and influential.* They select, synthesise *and compare* information from a variety of sources. (QCA website consultation version, 5 February 2007)

Yet teachers of English do need greater guidance in the ways that they should be assisting their able students to make progress. Most able students in English arrive at their secondary school already accomplished readers. Few secondary teachers have ever been trained in the teaching of reading, and they have only a limited knowledge of what 'progression' might mean in reading. Such topics rarely appear on PGCE programmes of study for training secondary teachers. The sorts of criteria outlined above – even in the updated version – contribute only in limited ways to teachers' attempts to move their readers to another, improved level.

One major area of concern for teachers of more able English students in Key Stage 3 is their sense that the test administered to all students at the end of Year 9 is simply unworthy of their most successful groups. While a few of the questions are open-ended and invite responses commensurate with the ability of the more able, they are not the main matter of the test. Most of the content is sited at the point of low-level comprehension, incapable of offering worthwhile insights into the progress and engagement of the young people involved, and tracking the many intellectual gains they may have been making.

In the autumn of 2006 the government began to suggest an approach to testing that would mean it could be conducted at times when it might be deemed suitable, rather than at the end of each Key Stage as happens at present. The Gilbert Review of education, commissioned by the DfES to explore in depth the notion of personalised learning, reporting in December 2006 makes an open plea:

> Recently, many secondary schools have increased the number of pupils entered early for national assessments and public examinations, enabling them to progress at a pace that matches their learning better. We believe there is a case for increasing further the flexibility of national assessment to enable all pupils to demonstrate their level of achievement when they are ready. (DfES 2006)

While this suggestion has the advantage of getting the test 'out of the way', it raises serious questions about what departments offer as alternative programmes both before and after the actual test. Those students who are accelerated to sit the test at the end of Year 8 should not be subjected to a curriculum actually reduced in quality, focused more on the test than it might have otherwise been. Similarly, the most common curriculum of too many English departments in Key Stage 4 is a limited study of the texts to be examined at GCSE when the students reach the age of 16. If these 'fast-tracked' students are then merely subjected to a three-year period of study of the same limited few texts, rather than the two-year model, they will have accrued no benefit from such a re-arrangement.

Being properly aware of the more able students as they arrive in their secondary school is an essential prerequisite for quickly getting under way with, and gaining the most from, an appropriate programme, however long the students spend in Key Stage 3. Establishing a rich and broad-reaching collection of study aims in Key Stage 4, requiring much more than a working familiarity with a small set of texts, is the most effective way to build on such a start.

Ensuring the best learning opportunities for more able students

The 5-year secondary English curriculum

Most English departments in secondary schools usually provide two separate programmes of study for the period of compulsory education with only the minimum of planned overlap. One programme, lasting three years, for students aged 11 to 14, usually comprises units of about six weeks duration (roughly equivalent to a school half term), including, towards its conclusion, study of a Shakespeare play. The scheme of work (SoW) for such a programme will include some activities familiarising the students with examples of poetry, separate works of prose, occasionally a dramatic text and studying media-based materials. There will also be regular practice of the test administered to all students at the end of the Key Stage. The second SoW, for students aged 14 to 16, is mostly intended to ensure that learners are familiarised with the contents of, and likely questions that might be asked about, one or two works of prose, an anthology of poetry and a couple of dramatic works, including a Shakespeare play. The students will also, in both Key Stages, be encouraged to write creatively and for different purposes in a number of contexts.

What is really missing from this arrangement is a longitudinal sense of learning that embraces the final five years of statutory education. It is rare to discover an English department that has found time to stand aside from the many demands imposed on subject teams nationally during the past decade and be able to redesign a substantial learning curriculum for its students aged 11 to 16. At best, any learning overview that may exist does so only over the extent of single Key Stages. Yet planning likely to advantage all students properly starts at the 'long-term stage'. Effective planning needs the stability of a programme designed to bring about 'deep learning', as described by John West-Burnham, which establishes a genuine sense of progression.

Long-term planning for progression

'Long-term planning' in the context understood in this book refers to the whole programme for English over a period of five years, from entry to secondary school, aged 11, to the conclusion of GCSE, aged 16 – a period that should be regarded as a linked entity.

On the CD accompanying this book is a suggested outline curriculum development pro forma, or template, for 'long-term planning' not currently familiar to English teachers. It comprises two interweaving strands. The vertical strands roughly equate to the sorts of learning packages or units currently familiar to English teachers: 'poetry', 'moving image', narrative fiction, prose, etc. The horizontal strands are a new development, and depend on the department's own view and vision of the subject. These 'strands' are not as recognisable or usual as the more concrete unit titles, but have to do with more abstract intellectual approaches to the subject which can be improved and progressed. If I was an English curriculum leader, I would be keen to see my students developing their understanding of 'rhetoric', for instance. 'Rhetoric', or persuasive language, is firmly embedded in a huge variety of text types. Over the five-year span of their study in my department, I would want students increasingly to be aware of and more readily recognise and reflect on the different examples of rhetorical texts they encounter. Another strand might have to do with 'the poetic'. This area of understanding would involve much more than merely studying poetry; it would also be about students becoming more confident about identifying the prodigious use of imagery and the metaphoric, or close attention to very precise language, for instance, in our language. A third strand might be devoted to paying attention to commonplace, standard, unusual or unique grammatical features evident in textual materials being read.

The real point of these 'horizontal strands' is that English teachers would be encouraged to focus more closely on ways in which they could fashion learning units to bring about tangible progression over a number of textual encounters. Their inclusion would invite English departments to design a curriculum which bears its own hallmark, and which might be developed to include particular interests of the members of that department. This way of approaching planning could be very beneficial for more able students, as the sorts of suggested strands are open-ended, and would allow for a degree of progression dependent on the capacities and abilities of the individual learner. Setting up this way of thinking about planning the subject has the potential of re-energising professional engagement, which has deteriorated badly as a result of perceived government prescription and directing since the late 1980s.

Medium-term planning with a focus on learning

There is no absolute definition of 'medium-term' planning. The term applies to different lengths of time in different schools. Some regard 'medium term' as comprising either the whole of Key Stage 3 (three years) or Key Stage 4 (two years), or single years within each Key Stage. Considering a whole Key Stage at a time offers more flexibility to the inspired curriculum planner, as in any one year most departments usually manage to study no more than six substantial units of work, each of between 15 and 20 working hours. Key Stage 3 has the potential of offering 15 or so different units, allowing for examination revision time and other distracting demands, but most students need to revisit areas of learning regularly, so some repetition of units is necessary. But even building a programme of work for a three-year period – with repeated units – still allows for the planning of substantial progression.

Long-term English planning

Units of learning

A blank long-term English planning grid. Columns are organised by year (Year 7, Year 8, Year 9, Year 10, Year 11), each divided into units of learning. Rows list the strands of progression.

Units of learning by year:

- **Year 7:** fictional prose; poetry; moving-image/visual literacy; non-fiction/information texts; drama; print media; wider reading/writing for pleasure/multi-modal
- **Year 8:** fictional prose; poetry; moving-image/visual literacy; non-fiction/information texts; drama; print media; wider reading/writing for pleasure/multi-modal
- **Year 9:** fictional prose; poetry; moving-image/visual literacy; non-fiction/information texts; drama; KS3 SAT; wider reading/writing for pleasure/multi-modal
- **Year 10:** fictional prose; poetry; drama; moving-image; wider reading/writing for pleasure
- **Year 11:** fictional prose; poetry; drama; moving-image; wider reading/writing for pleasure

strands of progression:

- rhetoric (persuasion + ideology)
- the poetic
- narrative
- the dramatic
- the intertextual
- analysis + response
- literacy/purpose (grammar)
- digital technologies
- genre
- changing language
- future needs

Most English departments have put together a folder containing a 'medium-term' unit of work, such as the 'Year 8 poetry unit'. Few would be able to track worthwhile progression about *poetry learning* across the three separate poetry units provided for Year 7, Year 8 and Year 9. Even fewer still have planned that progression on as the starting point for progression into Years 10 and 11. The same situation would also be found in many departments in respect of, for instance, media texts. However, more able students need such a framework if they are to realise their goals and make the sort of progress of which they are truly capable. They should be able to build on previous learning and set up new directions of study that lead them regularly into unexplored learning territory. A medium-term plan without a learning direction or a distinctive identity as a component in a learning journey is a rather hollow instrument.

To contribute to a better focus on *learning*, I always suggest to the English departments I support that they employ a distinctively tightly focused vocabulary. It is becoming very usual these days to visit classrooms where teachers have published on some central notice space the 'objectives' or purpose of the lesson. Dylan Wiliam and Paul Black's research (1998) makes an indisputable case for fully articulating the intended learning with students, but the manner of that articulation is not always sufficiently securely focused to bring about the genuine learning desired. Shirley Clarke, a researcher who explores Wiliam and Black's ideas in real classrooms, probes this situation helpfully in the following:

> There is still a need to sort out learning intentions at the planning stage. Too many learning intentions are in fact activities and contain the context of the learning. Deciding success criteria for muddled learning intentions, focusing the lesson and subsequent feedback is problematic. It doesn't help that many of the QCA SoW learning objectives are muddled in this way. When learning intentions are 'pure', context free, the success criteria work like a dream, the lesson focuses appropriately and the feedback is obvious. Most importantly, the connections are made clear for the children; the learning intention can apply to a number of contexts. (Clarke 2003)

The vocabulary of the various government sponsored documents, such as the Key Stage 3 Framework (DfEE 2001), outlining Schemes of Work in English does not immediately lend itself to focused learning attention. Pupils are expected to 'work out'; 'read accurately'; 'investigate'; 'recognise and use'; 'draw links between'; 'select and present'; or take part in other such busy engagements. All of this language is conveyed in terms of activities, not pointing to the actual learning that should be resulting as an outcome of the activities that will have taken place. So, in Year 7, in the 'Reading' column of the Framework, sub-paragraph 'Study of literary texts', pupils should be taught to:

> 19. explore how form contributes to meaning in poems from different times and cultures, e.g. *storytelling in ballads*

To enable this area of study to become more firmly centred on learning, the teacher has to make a quick mental re-adjustment to foreground the actual learning intended from these lessons. I would firmly recommend that teachers preface all such 'learning intentions' with the words 'to know' or 'to understand'. These are verbs of a different order from those cited above. They are not merely activities – suggesting things to be done – but cognitive framings, establishing what is to be

Medium-term English Planning: Year 7

Autumn Term

Introductory Unit

Learning Unit 1 (e.g. fictional prose)	Learning Unit 2 (e.g. moving image)
Key learning intention:	Key learning intention:
Strands of progression:	Strands of progression:
1.	1.
2.	2.
3.	3.

Wider Reading

Spring Term

Learning Unit 3 (e.g. poetry)	Learning Unit 4 (e.g. print media)
Key learning intention:	Key learning intention:
Strands of progression:	Strands of progression:
1.	1.
2.	2.
3.	3.

Wider Reading

Summer Term

Learning Unit 5 (non-fiction/information)	Learning Unit 6 (drama)	Learning Unit 7
Key learning intention:	Key learning intention:	Key learning intention:
Strands of progression:	Strands of progression:	Strands of progression:
1.	1.	1.
2.	2.	2.
3.	3.	3.

Wider Reading

English for Gifted and Talented Students. SAGE © Geoff Dean 2008

A framework for looking at texts

1 Who speaks this text?

Is there an 'I' or a 'we' in the text?
What kind of voice is this?
Does the writer address me directly, or through an adopted 'persona'?

2 Who is being spoken to?

Is there a 'you' in the text?
What kind of audience is being addressed, and how can we tell?
Am I prepared to include myself in this audience?

3 Where does this text come from?

What do we know about when, why and how it was produced?
Does the text itself disclose these things?
What status does it have?
What values does the text assume?

4 What kind of text is this?

What other texts does it remind me of?
What form does it take?
What recognisable conventions has the writer adopted?)

5 What does the text want?

What do I deduce about the writer's intentions?
Are these intentions openly stated?
What kind of reading does this text invite?

6 What does this text mean to me?

What are my motives as a reader of this text?
How have I chosen to interpret it?
Do I share its values?
What thoughts has it prompted?
You might like to ask all these questions of the page you are holding.

The resources of written texts

In discussing these questions, it might be helpful to consider some detailed *rhetorical choices* which writers make:

- Presentational: e.g. choices of lay-out, type-face, illustration;
- Organisational: e.g. choices of narrative, logical, metrical or figurative pattern;
- Grammatical: e.g. choices of tense, mode, person, syntax, punctuation;
- Lexical: e.g. choices of vocabulary, idiom, metaphor.

From LINC materials, 1992

learned. In the classroom, the study suggestion quoted above will need to be expressed in something like the following manner, if it is to qualify as a true learning intention:

> To know that form contributes to meaning (in this instance through studying story-telling in ballads from different times and cultures).

This detail may seem trivial and finicky on first consideration, but it actually matters a great deal, and teachers thinking habitually in this manner will shape and mould learning for their classes more effectively, and with improved results. The real learning we want students to take from this particular work and other related work is that *form contributes to meaning*. There are almost limitless ways in which that particular intention can be impressed on learners, through many different textual examples. The ballads, and their selection from a range of times and cultures, are just one of many possible ways of approaching the central learning – but it is the *learning* that is really important, not the examples of sorts of text through which the learning will be discovered and embedded. This detailed attention begins to make teachers shift their priorities from coverage of certain areas of activity towards what the true priorities for learning might then be in a mature English curriculum. The purpose of the National Curriculum is to ensure that students enjoy a full entitlement coverage of areas of study. Teachers, however, should be determining what their students need to learn, and devising a programme that makes that learning as pronounced and successful as possible. Having identified the most relevant learning intentions and engaged the students, teachers then should establish assessable success criteria able to inform students how effective their learning has been.

All students, according to the National Curriculum for English should study poetry written both before and after 1914. This does not mean that there has to be a poetry unit in every school's English curriculum. The department might choose to study poetry in all sorts of contexts that better enable students to have a more secure understanding of what is to be learned. Similarly, all other areas of coverage can be reconfigured in many possible packages. At the end of the course, however, which is five years long, the department should be satisfied that its students have achieved a significant amount of learning about English – its language and the manifestations in which that language is exemplified – to put their learning to effective communicative use, and to make them confident and excellent meaning-makers of all the texts they will subsequently encounter.

If all the above is necessary to contribute more powerfully to the eventual success for all students in secondary education – which it is – then such approaches are even more necessary to bring about the best provision for that group considered to be the most able. Their learning should be substantial and appropriately wide-ranging, but also capable of being developed in ways the learner can determine. They need to know very precisely what they are expected to be learning, so that they can become practised partners in the process of creating worthwhile success criteria. They should be quite capable, after proper induction, of suggesting ways in which their learning can be 'proved' or substantially demonstrated.

Learning in reading

Worthwhile learning intentions to plan for and teach

1   To know the typical characteristics of … (an author) and/or … (a genre)

2   To know the differences between novels written before … and the postmodern novel

3   To know how characters are established and developed in …

4   To understand the structural devices employed by …

5   To know the main concerns being explored by … in their novels/stories etc

6   To know the differences between novels and short stories

7   To understand how meaning is made through different structural devices in the poems of …

8   To be able to explain the dramatic features of …

9   To understand the development of … in the works of …

10 To explain the distinctive features of …

11 To compare and contrast the … of … and …

Short-term plans with a focus on learning

When a department has constructed its medium-term plan, there should – properly – be a substantial overriding and guiding learning intention that holds the plan together and gives it focus and purpose; e.g.

> To know the features and characteristics of 'gothic texts', and to be able to recognise and describe these in unfamiliar examples;

or

> To know that postmodern authors (those publishing towards the end of the twentieth century and beyond) are writing to have different intended effects on their audiences than authors publishing in Victorian times;

or

> To know that film language is being conveyed through a number of different effects (e.g. lighting, sound, *mise-en-scène*, editing), and to recognise and explain what these devices are adding to the meaning of … [film title(s)]

(I hope that it is becoming clear that these sorts of learning intentions already begin to offer the outlines of the success criteria that will show some of the aspects of learning.)

The separate lessons of the unit will then all be led by sub-learning intentions, contributing to the key learning intention. So a sub-learning intention that a teacher might suggest early in the study of the first example above might be:

> To know the significant features of the 'gothic' period, and why it came about.

This 'sub-learning intention' could reasonably occupy up to three lessons of the whole unit. Some small assessment or probing activity might then take place to discover how much of that learning has been truly absorbed by the students. More able students should be very confident about what they know – which they could have discovered in different degrees of independence.

This sub-learning intention would then be succeeded by a further one, and so on, until the unit reached its conclusion. At that stage, two or three lessons would be earmarked at the conclusion of the module to enable the full demonstration, in a number of different ways, or media, by groups or individuals (not just through written essays) of how much genuine learning had occurred.

Further reading

Bowring-Carr, Christopher and John West-Burnham (1997) *Effective Learning in Schools*. London: Pearson Education.

Dean, Geoff (2004) *Improving Learning in English*. London: David Fulton.

5

Personalisation and other Support Structures in English

What personalisation might mean in English and how it could be of benefit to more able students

What this chapter is about

This chapter considers the increasingly important idea of 'personalisation', and what it might mean in English in respect to more able students. Professor David Hargreaves' interpretation of this idea suggests that personalising teaching and learning can be realised through nine interconnecting 'gateways':

> learning to learn
> assessment for learning
> new technologies
> advice and guidance
> mentoring
> student voice
> organisation
> workforce reform
> curriculum

Defining personalisation

During the last three years, ministers of state and other agencies concerned with education have been increasingly interested in the developing notion of 'personalisation'. 'Personalisation' is a concept not just applicable in education but also relevant in a number of public services, or any service where large numbers of people are being catered for at one time. Traditionally, state education has been designed more on a 'one size fits all' model, where the individual is expected to fit the system. So, in its present manifestation education is a service in which everybody attends school at the same time; the lessons are a standard length; there is a National Curriculum guiding the areas of study for all; external examinations are conducted at the same chronological points in each student's life; and lessons, which usually take place in the educational institution, are designed mostly for whole classes. Yet, in the real world, people develop intellectually, socially and emotionally at different rates; they learn in a variety of different ways and places; their needs are never the same; and their goals are hugely diverse.

Personalisation is an organising approach (not a new, stand-alone initiative) which draws together a number of recent areas of improvement in schools, with the intention of offering more focused attention to individual students. It does not promise a one-to-one teacher–student relationship – such an arrangement would not be possible within the capacity of the education system, however desirable. However, it could bring about circumstances in which each learner enjoys more choice of courses and content; more control of their learning; greater flexibility in the times of learning and sources of information; and more precise starting points based on personal previous experiences. It should also mean that learners accept and enjoy far greater responsibility for their own learning, replacing the current 'dependency culture' of the more traditional school classroom.

Of course, there would need to be massive shifts in both the culture and practice of education for such radical developments to come about exactly as described above. The wholesale changing of current expectations and a fundamental change in the understanding of parents, employers, and universities would be required, just to begin bringing about any chance of minimal implementation and realisation of this initiative. Yet, smaller, more manageable features and elements of personalisation could well be achieved in the near future if schools made only minor adjustments to the structures and organisation they currently take for granted, but changed their attitudes in a wholly different manner about the sorts of learning goals and the types of learners they intend projecting towards. And the most promising group of students with whom these elements could more profitably be explored and practised, in the first instance, are those identified as more able.

It is realistically possible for schools to move, in simple steps, toward personalisation, and even possible for individual departments within those schools to make some small degrees of discernible progress. David Hargreaves, the educational scholar, supported the Specialist Schools Trust to consider the implications of personalisation in a series of meetings in 2004/5 (www.clusterweb.org.uk/docs/ HargreavesPersonalisedLearning.pdf).

He sees personalising learning as

- a version of customisation in education;

- the core of educational transformation;

- involving incremental and radical innovation;

- demanding a new approach to development and research.

Hargreaves (2005) describes personalisation as a process that

•   reinforces some current practices;

•   demands modification of some of these practices;

•   entails creating some new practices;

and suggests the following nine 'gateways' available to all schools through which the initial manoeuvres might be made.

The nine gateways to personalisation

Learning to learn

I have described elsewhere in this book the enormous value that can be gained by students understanding how they learn and how they can improve their learning, and being encouraged to articulate those personal insights. This attitude means much more than just acknowledging and supporting a simplistic understanding of 'learning styles', as it has been adopted in a few schools, in which there is a concentration on oral, visual and kinaesthetic approaches to all lessons as if these alone were capable of enabling students to know themselves and their preferred styles of studying in all circumstances satisfactorily. (Frank Coffield, Professor of Education at the Institute of Education, has researched this topic extensively and reached more than sceptical conclusions about its limited effects: *Education Guardian*, 4 May 2004 and 31 May 2005.)

In its more sophisticated manifestation, students are expected to consider their attitudes to work, the conditions which enable them to work more purposefully, how they handle distraction and delaying tactics, strategies that bring about re-engagement, and ways of evaluating how focused and successful the learner might be relative to the criteria describing the intended learning outcomes. This coherent approach can be the result of students determining to take responsibility for and control of their learning circumstances. They need to be self-motivated and determined to succeed.

Some schools have already adopted 'learning to learn' schemes, such as the Building Learning Power programme, based on the research and recommendations of Guy Claxton and his colleagues at the University of Bristol. Students are beginning to discover that they can organise their approaches to work more effectively and efficiently if they have a clearer idea of their own dispositions. Do they work systematically, or are they 'immediate deadline beaters'? Do they work best sitting at a desk, or lounging on a bed or settee? Do they make notes, gathering all the necessary material together, or do they adopt a 'bigger picture overview', constantly revisiting their written work and adding and refining each time? These, and a huge host of similar considerations, are the material of knowing oneself as a learner, and their clear articulation and understanding can lead to improved results, by those determined to act appropriately on their findings.

Assessment for Learning

Many schools have been developing an increasingly refined approach to assessment for learning (or AfL) during the last five years. Much of this interest is based on the research of Professors Dylan Wiliam and Paul Black, at various times heads of the assessment unit of Kings College, London, and published in their series of booklets beginning with *Inside the Black Box: Raising Standards through Classroom Assessment* (1998), concerned with using assessment methods designed to improve learning, rather than merely to measure it. They make a strong case about ways of improving students' learning based on comprehensive areas of knowledge about individual learners. Too often, they claim, work is planned from a point which is not always appropriate for the learners involved, or fails to address the range of needs of individuals in any one classroom.

Since the introduction of end of Key Stage tests, or SATs, in the 1990s, schools have become far better informed about the broad levels of achievement of their students, and this information has been fed back to teachers to help them plan relevant tasks at the correct level. But this more focused way of using the available data is by no means practised universally, and greater individualisation based on this data is still necessary in many circumstances. A large number of schools now purchase predictive services, such as MidYIS (Middle Years Information System, YELLIS (Year 11 Information System) and Alis (Advanced level Information System) to enable teachers to have a realistic idea about the examination potential of separate cohorts. They also receive statistical information from the Fischer Family Trust, referring closely to the examination potential of individual students. All of this information should be contributing to the decision-making processes behind planning the best possible appropriate English lessons, ensuring that they closely meet the learners' needs.

But 'Assessment for Learning' needs to be more broad-ranging and generous in its definition than just being about the statistical data related to examination and test outcomes. It should also embrace students' interests and preferences across a number of learning characteristics. English is a natural subject in which to explore the notion of personalisation. In any class of students there will be, for instance, a huge range of reading interests and abilities. A teacher planning work in an area of the curriculum based, as it so often is, on a single text, will be considerably empowered by being aware of the reading tastes and attainment of the whole class. This knowledge could then contribute to drawing up a range of more tailored approaches to the core text, the possibility of individual readers developing their work and understanding in different directions, and collectively contributing a number of important insights and learning that would simply not have been even considered without such a platform. The sharing of all the different possible responses to that core text that might be harvested from any group of students could lead to significantly greater understanding about the text than has been possible in other circumstances.

Teachers also need to know how competent and confident their students are as presenters and writers of what they understand, to allow them both to set up demonstrations of their progress in the appropriate media and devices that illustrate those strengths, but also to challenge them in areas where they need greater regular practice. Knowing what we do about students should always be a useful tool in two ways: to give us knowledge about the 'comfort zone' of our students and what might constitute effective levels of challenge; and to know those areas where they ought to be making better progress than that they currently display.

New technologies

English teachers have much to learn about the ways in which technologies can play a potentially significant part in the learning of their students. In considerable numbers of schools, technology is still only tentatively employed by English staff, or the learning activities in which technology is incorporated lack real challenge, often lagging behind the students' own expertise. Access to computer technology for whole-class use is also a major matter of concern in too many schools.

A great many young people in secondary schools have accrued considerable ICT skills by the time they transfer from their primary schools at the age of 11, and this phenomenon is growing exponentially. A huge proportion of students who are more able in English are especially comfortable with the technology available in their schools, and many have logged hundreds of hours in an already wide and growing collection of computer-based activities. They are at ease with the overlapping potentials of audio and visual digital materials, and the ways that such texts can potentially be related to the sorts of written texts usually promoted in English classrooms. A large proportion will be familiar with, and sometimes avid fans of, many computer games and narrative-driven activities, requiring a large repertoire of language-based skills. Others will know about programs designed to draw together a range of design and presentational tools, capable of adding extra meaning and depth to a large range of textual outcomes. There will be young people in our schools who quite naturally and unremarkably employ devices such as laptop computers, 'tablets' and hand-held appliances, on which to make their notes, outlines of written work and other ways of capturing thinking and creativity. These learners will not be overwhelmed by the increasing power of technology, and will understand the ways in which it can be used to challenge current practices and move thinking in new directions.

New technology may well have other significant effects in the very near future. In an article in the *Guardian's* Technology section (5 October 2006), the writer discussed the imminent widespread availability of electronic books, handheld computers able to hold up to 140,000 titles. Such devices, which will enable students easily to conduct some very sophisticated linguistic research, are likely to change reading practices hugely and bring about a different relationship between reader and text of a kind that has been little discussed. This example is merely one tiny illustration of the massively changed textual landscape that will be freely available in the next decade.

> Everyone agrees: the school of the future will be radically different from the model of the last 130 years. Technology will ensure that. (Bennett 2005)

Discussing with more able English students some of the potential learning areas they can already see for themselves will provide a good starting point towards change, and one which will, initially, require few resources or already worked examples. Indeed, from such discussions and explorations, English teachers could well be pointed towards the possible new devices and programs they should be considering incorporating in their work in the very near future, and their own training requirements capable of enabling them to service such developments.

English teachers will need to be humble about allowing their more able students to demonstrate to them the sorts of advanced skills and abilities they have already acquired. A reliable way of developing one's own skills is to be able to teach others, and able students should be encouraged to 'teach' their teachers in areas of mutual interest. I know of students who have moved on to university with really impressive technological accomplishments, which were completely unknown to their schools and had never been sought for at any stage. It is not acceptable that students' capabilities are so poorly acknowledged by their schools, and it is little wonder that many feel bored and not properly catered for in the secondary stages of their education. There is really no time to wait on this issue. It is a matter that needs immediate and serious action.

Advice and guidance

Personalisation is not about encouraging learners to have the flexibility to explore all sorts of unsupervised, free choice activities, at the whim of each individual. As already explained above, it offers a way of approaching study that can only work effectively when the monitoring teachers have a really clear sense of the abilities and capabilities of their students. They will also need to be able to estimate the most appropriate areas in the subject in which their students are likely to achieve the greatest successes, relative to their goals.

Teachers will need to give relevant and focused advice to students, yet also allow sufficient room for young people, ultimately, to make their own decisions about the domains in which they wish to study. Successful teachers will move into roles more like that of adviser and coach, guiding students through prompting and careful suggestions. They will need to develop the advanced skills of articulating what is available for their students to choose, while not directing that choice too firmly. 'Advice and guidance' fully comes into its own as a core component of personalisation when students have genuine choices to make, and yet might be unpractised in making them. Really successful schools of the future will be those which, among other qualities, are able to offer a sufficiently broad range of alternatives that students are able to choose 'pathways' which suit their many differing needs and interests.

Mentoring

Mentoring is a further step on from advice and guidance, and should be made available, as a matter of course, for all students regarded as more able. It is different from 'advice and guidance' in that it pays less attention to working out directions and purposes of study, and offers a support programme designed to ensure that the student makes the best possible progress within areas of study already selected. Learners may be encountering problems in finding resources; they might be finding relationships with peers or teachers difficult for various reasons; they might be encountering problems with their work patterns or places of learning. These would be appropriate grounds for students to seek support from a mentor and discuss possible solutions to the matters being addressed. Mentors might also be able to 'champion' those they supervise in certain circumstances, and link their mentees to bigger or more relevant programmes of which they are aware.

Not all mentoring has to be problem-related. Mentors also play a valuable role by celebrating successes already achieved, and encouraging, through confirmation and endorsement, those being mentored along routes or directions they are beginning to discover for themselves. Effective mentoring will be allied with some of the same principles of 'learning to learn', focused as it could be on encouraging learners to take a more self-evaluative position in relation to their studies.

Student voice

Any movement towards personalisation has to acknowledge and pay real attention to the voices of the participants. Many of the other components of the overall personalisation programme, or 'gateways', make serious re-thinking of the secondary English curriculum very necessary, but for 'student voice' to be wholly effective a really massive change in the subject English will be essential.

While it will be the continuing duty of schools to ensure that all students are properly literate and able to operate successfully in the world because they possess and are confident with the requisite language skills, a personalised English programme will, by definition, offer much greater individual choice to each student within clearly structured areas of entitlement. Prescribing a list of set texts will not be appropriate and, in many respects, the whole content of any future English curriculum will have to be far more flexible to allow and make possible the sorts of textual configurations students may wish to nominate. Students are likely to want to choose a far greater range of possible textual sources than is currently possible, and across a much wider landscape of available media. Of course, their ability to know some of the possible related links and associations will depend on teachers' knowing what possible 'pathways' could be chosen, which would be another of the functions of the 'advice and guidance' provision.

To have an idea of what I am suggesting in this section, it might be helpful to consider a study unit exploring, for instance, the development of detective fiction. Reading books such as Conan Doyle's Sherlock Holmes series and making a comparison with Wilkie Collins' *The Moonstone* could well be where the study begins. In more modern times, the 'Rebus' series by Ian Rankin or the Colin Dexter 'Morse' books would be excellent comparators. But, of course, these texts do not only exist in book form, they are also the subject of many films and television series. The representations of Sherlock Holmes in moving image alone would give any interested learner massive amounts of fascinating material to study. As with filmic versions of Shakespeare plays, so each generation imprints its own values and cultural preoccupations on the interpretations of the character of Sherlock Holmes, and the ways his stories are told in different times, over the period of the last century to the present day. So, the Hollywood versions of the 1930s and 1940s, often starring Basil Rathbone and Nigel Bruce, are vastly different from the Jeremy Brett and Edward Burke television productions of the 1980s and 1990s, and would – of themselves – be excellent material for consideration. There have also been various collections of radio plays, featuring different pairings in the central roles, easily accessible on CDs and adding importantly to the available study material.

In addition, there might be the additional comparison of such films as those featuring, for instance, Charlie Chan, the 'Thin Man' series, the more contemporary *Bullitt, The French Connection* and the 'Dirty Harry' films, as well as the novels of Dashiell Hammett and Raymond Chandler, the graphic novels involving Dick Tracy and *Sin City*, the television programmes involving Taggart and Jane Tennison, and computer games involving some of these and other well-known characters in this genre. It would be possible, through a personalised approach, to introduce the generic topic of fictionalised detectives to any number of classes, and then support an infinite number of unique study programmes along 'pathways' chosen by the individual students.

'Student voice' also means students being asked for their views and attitudes about the provision made by the educating institution, the levels of support, the understanding of how genuinely 'independent learning' is being interpreted, and other important considerations about which students might have views. Other meanings will involve the students being fully represented on the student council, the curriculum and examination, and governing boards.

Organisation

In the early years of the twenty-first century, most students attend timetabled English lessons, meaning that they are expected to turn up to lessons at the same times on a number of similar occasions each week or each fortnight (depending on whether the school's timetable works on a weekly or two-weekly cycle) over the period of a school year. This is how programmes of lessons are organised in virtually every secondary school in England, and other countries. Moving towards personalisation will require schools to reconsider that method of uniform systematic organisation, and accept that alternative ways of organising learning in English might be possible and, even, more advantageous.

Certainly, students will need to meet with their teachers fairly regularly, but not necessarily every week at the same times. Teachers will probably want to share some lead lessons with larger groups of students, for instance, when new topics are introduced, or being evaluated. Larger groups of students might need to meet together again, under the supervision of teachers, when students are making presentations at the end of a topic. And there could well be other times when such meetings are deemed appropriate and necessary. Yet, for the majority of time assigned to most topics of study it should not be essential for students to be under the direct control of teachers.

After the initial period of establishing a new unit, students should be capable of spending time in individual, paired or group study, depending on the numbers of peers sharing their particular topics. It might be that a Teaching Assistant (or whatever name such personnel will be called in the future) would be available at agreed times, or the actual teachers can be contacted to consult over matters of detail, or to offer specialist advice when required. But such provision could well be provided online, or through texting or other available mobile telephone contact. It is likely that the teachers would want to set up an arrangement for 'tutorials', conducted with individuals or a small number of students to ensure that study is up-to-date, relevant and properly challenging, but these would not need to be arranged more often than every few weeks.

A completely new departure for most schools seeking to establish genuine personalisation will be through the adoption of 'learning platforms', which help to make flexible organisation more feasible. 'Learning platform' is an umbrella term used to cover software whose core role is to manage learning materials for students. They give every learner access to personal online web space, where they can store course work and their achievements. They also give every teacher access to teaching resources and tools to support planning and information sharing. In addition, these platforms support 'personalised learning' by enabling teachers to tailor the curriculum to individual learners' needs. Yet again, it will be very necessary for teachers to be adept with technological skills, and to concentrate on exploring the potential of these systems.

Such a radical deviation from current practice will not come about easily, but will need to be scrutinised, planned and worked towards as an intended goal during the course of the next decade. Teachers will need to be more prepared to hand over areas of responsibility to their learners, and to enable that responsibility to grow seriously with a minimum of supervisory contact. A few secondary schools are already, in the first decade of the century, exploring more flexible arrangements when older students are expected to attend at agreed times, but by no means every day. This model will need further experimentation before anything like a routine is fully established, but English teachers could make it work more quickly and more effectively with a positive and supporting attitude.

Workforce reform

It is not possible to contemplate what is likely to happen in education during at least the next decade without giving some attention to the potential changing workforce arrangements. About a third of current teachers will retire from or otherwise leave the profession in the next seven years, putting a huge strain on the remaining staff. At the same time there has been a significant increase in the numbers of support personnel recruited by schools since the Labour government formed its first modern administration in 1997. This decline in teacher numbers and growth in support people is gradually being recognised in the changing status of various roles. Some of the best Teaching Assistants, as they are known in most schools, are being encouraged by their senior staff to train for higher level qualifications, which will allow them to adopt a greater part of the teaching role in their schools. Other staff are training to be qualified mentors, and will be sufficiently skilled to offer that support directly to students.

It might not be science fiction to anticipate schools where teachers are regarded as 'learning managers', ultimately responsible for very large groups of youngsters, and presenting 'lead lessons', i.e. those which set students off on a new venture or course of research. While that unit is under way, however, the students might well be supported on a day-to-day basis by 'learning technicians', or perhaps 'learning mentors', who would be the equivalent of today's Teaching Assistants. Primary schools are already coming to terms with arrangements quite like those described above, and their inevitable spread into secondary schools has begun. With the growing association of some Teaching Assistants to different subject departments in the school, this sort of development is likely to develop further in the next few years. These 'learning technicians' or whatever they come to be known as, will be expected to model good learning strategies, even if they are not as specialist in their knowledge in any subject areas as their teacher colleagues.

Whatever the actual final position arrived at by schools – and there could well be a range of different staffing systems established in different areas – it is reasonable to realise that the traditional status quo will be impossible to sustain.

Curriculum

Of all the areas considered in this chapter, this component of personalisation has the greatest potential and the greatest set of potential problems.

The national school curriculum for English is hopelessly out of date. Even though it was devised in much like its current format in the late 1980s, it is still a curriculum essentially designed to prop up the recently disappeared remnants of the industrial revolution. It is a curriculum intended to provide the majority of people, the equivalent of the clerks and the book-keepers of the late industrial age, with just enough knowledge and information to operate in the workplace at a low level of supervision, without too much supervision. As we rush towards an information society at a rapid and exponentially accelerating rate, the educational system is in danger of becoming stranded in a position unlikely to enable satisfactory provision for learners who will be expected to work, make relationships and become successful citizens in the years from 2015 onwards.

In some respects, the study of literary English in the curriculum has moved on little since it was used to cover the gaping hole left by the decline of religion in the second part of the nineteenth century. The study of 'worthwhile literature' (a deliberately hazy notion) was first introduced into the English curriculum as an antidote to the inability of the church to provide answers to the nation's moral problems and a convincing riposte to its scientific developments. Terry Eagleton, in *Literary Theory: An Introduction*, claims:

> If one were asked to provide a single explanation for the growth of English studies in the later nineteenth century, one could do worse than reply: 'the failure of religion'. (Eagleton 1983)

He goes on to quote the inaugural address of an early professor of English Literature at Oxford, who stated baldly:

> England is sick, and … English literature must save it. The Churches (as I understand) having failed, and social remedies being slow, English literature has now the triple function: still, I suppose, to delight and instruct us, but also, and above all, to save our souls and heal the state. (Ibid.)

Matthew Arnold, an early exponent for the spread of literature (and an HMI inspector) had no doubts of literature's abilities to shape taste and judgement, advocating that children learn lines of 'great' poetry to enable them to become 'better citizens', less likely to indulge in the sorts of social revolution then common in mainland Europe. So English was seen as a civilising and moral force in its earliest incarnation in schools, and it clearly retained those purposes in the first English National Curriculum, introduced by the Conservative Party at the end of the 1980s. There is still a flavour of 'missionary work' in the introductory papers of many English department handbooks, with their intentions of 'raising the horizons' of their students by introducing them to great works of literature.

All students deserve the richest, most relevant curriculum that can possibly be provided: the more able students require a curriculum capable of establishing the sorts of learning experiences that truly demonstrate their current mettle and full potential. Unfortunately, this is not a situation that currently prevails in schools. And, even worse, we expect all our assessment practices at 14, 16 and 18 to be conducted through writing. There is no examination involving talk, and nothing that might test reading aloud and reading interpretation. Not remotely considered is the possibility that students might want to demonstrate their knowledge through other media: DVDs, CDs, PowerPoint, video or digital film. If 'personalisation' is to mean anything worthwhile in the future, our assessment systems will have to be radically overhauled to allow students to prove fully what they know, understand and can do in the ways that most convincingly showcase those talents.

English teaching has, during the past twenty years, been locked within one curriculum model and it is rare to hear of other possible alternatives. Yet, alternative ways of organising the English curriculum can and do exist. Gabrielle Cliff Hodges, writing in *EnglishDramaMedia* magazine in January 2006 summarises the suggestions of the American scholar in English Robert Scholes in his book *The Rise and Fall of English: Restructuring English as a Discipline* (1998). Scholes outlines what he calls 'a capstone course', suitable as he sees it for those about to leave school. I think that it has genuine possibilities as a most suitable course for the more able at a much earlier stage of their schooling. The course is about paying close attention to 'voices', with considerably different purposes, from the past and the present, with the final intention of making one's own voice heard. It gives real coherence to encountering the matter and materials of language. He proposes six units beginning with *Introduction to Voices of Modern Culture*, (voices are 'I', 'you' and 'me'), and proceeding through: *Stranger in the Village – Encountering the Other, being the Other* ('they' and 'I–they', 'us–them' relationships), *Cultures and Voices in a Single Text* (the multiplicity of voices and complexities of culture in one text), *Inheriting Earlier Voices* (study of a dramatic text in multiple ways over time), *Film Language and Culture* (analysis and making of film) and concluding with *Mediating Culture/the Representation of Events and People* (the process of mediation). This sort of educational thinking is light years away from the current secondary English programme in virtually every secondary school in the country, yet such integrated approaches would go a long way to addressing the current fragmented frameworks which stand in the way of effective learning.

Conclusion

Education in the twenty-first century will be very different. More able students in all schools should be major beneficiaries of this change as it involves paying greater attention to such minorities in a bigger 'inclusive' agenda, and the gradual implementation of personalised provision could be a significant step in that direction. English teachers and departments need to look carefully at the sorts of possibilities of change outlined in this chapter and determine what could be improved and developed without too much disruption or disturbance to their current programmes. Identifying just one small area of possible implementation – and there really are many – would be all that is required to begin an inevitable movement towards a much more fundamental change not too far away. With this approach it should be possible to look back in a year or so, and track an increasing trend of personalised provision, initially for the most able, but – ultimately – for the benefit of every learner in the subject.

Further reading

Scholes, R. (1998) *The Rise and Fall of English: Restructuring English as a Discipline.* New Haven & London: Yale University Press.

Wiliam, D. and Black, P. (1998) *Inside the Black Box: Raising Standards through Classroom Assessment.* London: King's College, London.

Activities to Support and Challenge More Able English Students in Secondary Schools

What this chapter is about

> It describes some of the many activities that more able students could be encouraged to pursue outside the normal curriculum requirements.
> It considers self-evaluation exercises which encourage the learners to consider their capabilities, background and aspirations.
> It outlines some broad reading, writing and speaking and listening experiences.

Starting points

Self-evaluation

The best possible starting point in deciding the programme for the most able is to begin from positions identified by the students themselves. Investing serious time and attention to asking pertinent and searching questions of themselves and their literacy/literary learning backgrounds is an important factor in ensuring that the next stages in their development are properly prepared. Over the long period I have worked alongside more able students, I have become increasingly convinced that to miss out this stage before considering 'where next?' is much like setting out on a difficult journey without a map.

What does self-evaluation in these circumstance look like? Quite simply, it comprises the raising and answering of a bank of straightforward questions to do with the literary/literacy/linguistic biographies and backgrounds of the students, so that they are in a strong position to describe themselves as engagers with language in all the varieties of ways they can reach for and imagine. Devoting special time to this activity at significant moments in students' school lives, such as when they first enter the school, move from year to year, or into a new key stage, cannot be recommended strongly enough. It is never wasted time and should be factored in to any planning as naturally as the different areas of selected learning. The teacher is able to learn invaluable information about individual learners, and the learners come to understand much about themselves, which contributes to their further learning.

Among typical components of the reading self-evaluation procedure are the following:

- What can you remember about learning to read?

- Who was the most important figure in your early reading development?

- Can you remember your earliest favourite texts, and which features made them so important or memorable?

- Which teachers have made an impression on you in your reading development?

- What was it that they did, or urged you to do, that made such an impression on you?

- Do you remember reading at home before you came to school?

- Which books did you constantly re-read, and why?

- Which texts do you particularly remember reading with real pleasure in pre-school/Key Stage 1/Key Stage 2?

- When did you begin to believe that you might be a more able reader, and what evidence did you have?

- How do you think your reading practices have changed since Key Stage 1/Key Stage 2?

- What are your current favourite sorts of texts? How broad are your reading tastes?

- What would you definitely never attempt to read? Why?

- What would you like to read, but have not yet found time?

- What other textual forms or media do you spend time on? What is your favourite textual medium? Have you considered why it might be?

- Are your reading habits, interests and tastes like any other students in the year?

- Whose recommendations about texts do you trust and, perhaps, respond to?

- What other information about texts gained outside school do you pay attention to?

- What do you think of the reading study conducted in English lessons?

Teachers could also use other self-evaluation tools at different stages to supplement these major self-evaluatory exercises. I have regularly employed a small collection of questions with classes that can be administered very quickly and simply at the beginning of each half term and immediately after the half term break, capable of maintaining a very simple record with at least six pieces of evidence every year. An example of this sheet and another from my colleague Simon Wrigley, English Adviser in Buckinghamshire, can be found on the accompanying CD.

Of course, teachers – and learners – are at liberty to devise any sort of questionnaire they wish. The real intent of this exercise is for learners to look much more carefully at their own behaviours in this area, to elicit possible patterns, to reconsider some habitual routines which could benefit from being challenged, to devise new reading intentions and to compare those issues that might be regarded as unproblematic with other learners. Teachers might also want to participate themselves, with worthwhile and interesting outcomes which they could share with their students.

The particular exercise illustrated above has dealt with only a limited area of reading. Making meaning in different textual materials calls for a range of related but different skills. Similar exercises can, and should, also be conducted to investigate students' writing and speaking expertise. If students are to contribute to the process of their own target-setting, they will need the good evidence and understanding of their own strengths and areas for possible development which is made more available through such enterprises.

Taking this sort of exercise seriously should have reciprocal benefits for English departments as well as for the students who put them to their own use. If a group of students comes to a collective agreement that an area of their linguistic development might be in need of much more attention, then areas of work and study could be planned to make good the shortfall. A 'listening' department will also be aware of what is being discovered from their students' enquiries and use that information as part of the review process of the current programmes.

Students participating in these activities will, of course, discuss their findings with their classmates, or other relevant students, and members of staff – possibly with their mentors. They will also record the findings in one way or another (it might be appropriate to represent the outcomes in a set of graphs, a PowerPoint presentation, or a short report) to use at a later stage relative to the next self-evaluation, to check progress and development.

Teachers should be ready to use this information as a necessary preamble to planning, because it qualifies as powerful evidence of *assessment for learning*.

Related, but appropriately different, questions should also be raised and used in a similar manner about students' writing background and current form. Students who

Reading Personality Questionnaire

Name   Date

1. What kinds of book would you choose to read?

	Always…sometimes…never				
	5	4	3	2	1
Adventure					
Historical					
Sports story					
School story					
Romance					
Detective/ mystery					
Horror					
Comedy					
Fantasy					
Animal					
Diary stories					
True life					
Poetry					
TV-related books					
Classics					

2. Where do you read?

	Always…sometimes…never				
	5	4	3	2	1
On the bus/ train					
In bed					
At school					
On the loo					
Other					

3. When do you read?

	Always…sometimes…never				
	5	4	3	2	1
10 mins here and there					
Filling in time					
Evenings					
Weekends					
Other					

4. How do you read?

	Always…sometimes…never				
	5	4	3	2	1
Every word					
Jump whole chunks					
Skim over boring bits					
Other					

5. Whom are you most likely to share or talk about books with?

	Always…sometimes…never				
	5	4	3	2	1
No one					
Friends					
Brother/sister					
Mum					
Teacher					
Other					

6. Why do you read – mainly?

Always...sometimes...never

	5	4	3	2	1
Fun					
School work					
Information					
Other					

7. Which book stands out in your memory?

Title

Author

Where & when read

How you felt

8. Which book have you most enjoyed reading in English lessons at school?

Title

Author

How you felt

9. How many hours do you think you read in a week on average?

0–1	1–4
4–7	7+

10. How do you search out a new book to read?

Always...sometimes...never

	5	4	3	2	1
Browse first few pages					
Read blurb					
Good front cover					
Friends' recommendation					
Family's recommendation					
Teacher's recommendation					
What's been on TV/film					
Other					

11. What do you do when you finish a really good book?

Always...sometimes...never

	5	4	3	2	1
Get another by same author a.s.a.p.					
Give it to a friend to read					
Read it again					
Other					

12. What are your reading habits?

Always...sometimes...never

	5	4	3	2	1
Read 2+ books at a time					
Remember authors					
Read for the pictures					
Read the end half way through					
Read just for the good bits					
Re-read					
Other					

13. How do you get reading books?

Always...sometimes...never

	5	4	3	2	1
Buy them					
Borrow from family					
Borrow from friends					
School library					
Public library					
Other					

14. Roughly how many books do you own?

Fewer than 10   10–50

50–100   100–200

200–500   More than 500

15. Is there a book you feel you should read, but know you never will?

Title

Author

16. How much time is timetabled each week in school for your own private reading?

0–15 mins

15–30 mins

30 mins –1 hour

More than 1 hour

17. What do you hope to have read/done by the end of this course/term?

18. Any other comments about your style of reading?

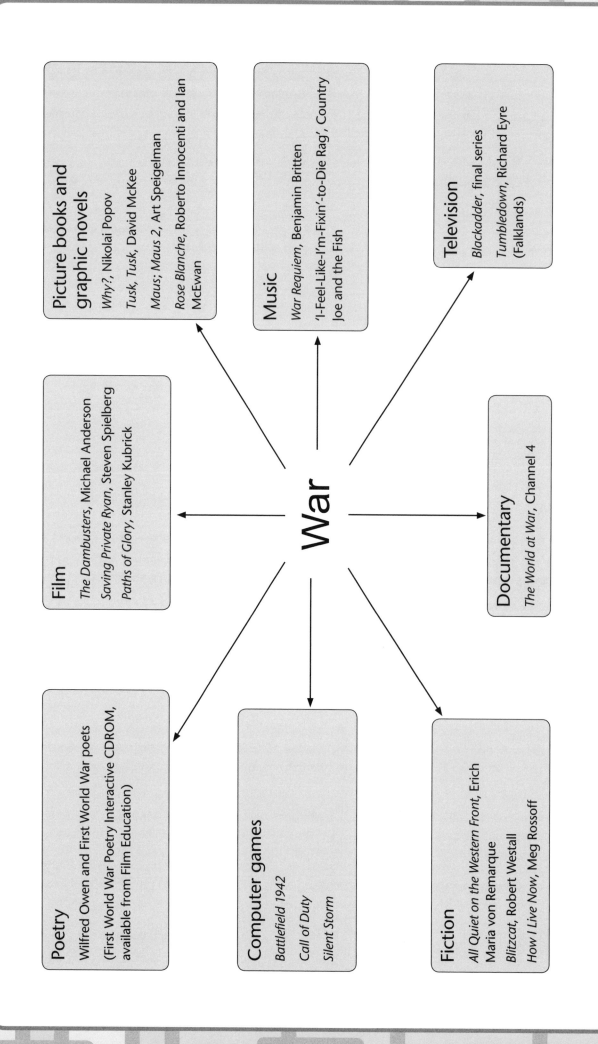

War

Picture books and graphic novels
Why?, Nikolai Popov
Tusk, Tusk, David McKee
Maus; Maus 2, Art Speigelman
Rose Blanche, Roberto Innocenti and Ian McEwan

Music
War Requiem, Benjamin Britten
'I-Feel-Like-I'm-Fixin'-to-Die Rag', Country Joe and the Fish

Television
Blackadder, final series
Tumbledown, Richard Eyre (Falklands)

Film
The Dambusters, Michael Anderson
Saving Private Ryan, Steven Spielberg
Paths of Glory, Stanley Kubrick

Documentary
The World at War, Channel 4

Poetry
Wilfred Owen and First World War poets
(First World War Poetry Interactive CDROM, available from Film Education)

Computer games
Battlefield 1942
Call of Duty
Silent Storm

Fiction
All Quiet on the Western Front, Erich Maria von Remarque
Blitzcat, Robert Westall
How I Live Now, Meg Rossoff

are respected and allowed to establish their own learning space in this manner are usually more prepared to study in more advanced ways, and continue to think more analytically about their subsequent endeavours.

Suggested activities to challenge and interest more able students in English

Activities for deeper learning with picture books

Until recently, the recommendation to use picture books with more able students in Key Stages 3 and 4 would have been met – at best – with a good deal of scepticism by many English teachers. Other, harsher, critics might have regarded such a tactic as a cheap stunt. Yet attitudes are changing, and these texts are now rarely regarded with disdain by older readers. Apart from those texts specifically designed for the very youngest readers, usually to support a particular stage in learning to read, most of these texts are really rich resources, capable of being employed in many circumstances, and can enable teachers of reading to move very quickly to the 'aboutness' of texts – what issues a text deals with. The acquisition of valuable reading 'knowledges' – i.e. understanding the many different issues at work in a text, which with longer texts only develops over many weeks of shared reading in classroom settings – can soon be equally well demonstrated as a result of reading picture texts in only a part of a short, single session.

Readers, for instance, need to develop confidence in realising and articulating that there can be more than one possible 'reading' of a text, and in becoming aware that complex texts are capable of being 'about' a number of ideas simultaneously. An excellent example is a text such as John Burningham's *Granpa* (1984). Able secondary readers will take only a few moments to work their way through the 221 words, although most would want to linger to consider carefully Burningham's very spare use of language and to investigate the illustrations with detailed assiduity. On virtually every page Burningham offers a single utterance from each of the two characters, but they are not consecutive, indeed, not obviously linked in any way. The reader is expected to fill in the gaps from all the other pictorial and written clues.

A further consideration might be for the teacher to ask the students if they could suggest what the text is 'about'. Alert readers might well come up with half a dozen possible suggestions:

- about relations between the generations

- about grandparenting

- about gaining experience

- about death and mourning

- about play and imagination

- about memories.

All of these themes would be merely a selection of the sensible speculative ideas students might reasonably offer. The learners should be reassured that all these suggestions are perfectly valid, and evidence for their inclusion in this discussion can be readily discovered in the text. The strongly attentive will also identify the changing of the seasons through the text: beginning in spring, the pictorial and narrative progression leads the reader to winter, when the grandfather dies.

Morag Styles, who lectures at Homerton College, Cambridge, describes picture books as 'polysemic texts', giving a sense of their possible richness and multi-layered value. Some gain impact by aligning the pictures in close harmony with the words on the page. Some 'work against' the illustrations, adding layers of enigma and further puzzlement for the readers. A few are wordless, requiring the pictures to convey all the meaning; in making sense of such texts readers will bring to the process all their previous knowledges. Whatever that relationship between reader and text, the very best picture texts deal with the same important issues of life and experience as their more wordy, 'chapter book' counterparts. Recent publications from Australia, such as *The Lost Thing* by Shaun Tan (2000), *The Viewer* by Gary Crew and Shaun Tan (1997), *Memorial* by Gary Crew and Shaun Tan (1999), *Tagged* (1997) and *The Water Tower* by Gary Crew and Steven Woolman (1994), are written specifically for students in secondary schools, dealing with matters such as the First World War, a horror story and a frightening character who challenges aspects of tolerance. These and other similar books illustrate many facets of postmodern texts, understanding which is an essential part of literacy knowledge for young people in the twenty-first century.

Possible uses of picture books for more able readers
- Re-reading texts that may have been childhood favourites:

    - to recall what the pleasures of early reading might have been;

    - to consider the sorts of meanings the older student might now be making of the text different from the meanings they would have made as infant readers;

    - to relate the text to other texts by the same author/illustrator and trace any discernible traits or themes perceived as developed over time;

    - to consider how the trends and tastes of picture books have changed.

- Exploration of significant 'issues': picture texts are able to focus very quickly on important matters in our lives, such as:

    - **conflict** – e.g. David McKee, *Tusk, Tusk* and *Three Little Monsters*; *Why*, a wordless text by Nikolai Popov;

- **tolerance** – e.g. *Oi, Get Off My Train,* John Burningham; *The Rabbits,* John Marsden and Shaun Tan;

- **gender matters** – e.g. *Piggybook,* Anthony Browne; *The Widow's Broom,* Chris Van Allsburg;

- **anger and rage** – e.g. *Not Now Bernard,* David McKee; *Where the Wild Things Are,* Maurice Sendak;

- **ideologies** – e.g. *Feathers and Fools,* Mem Fox; *Where the Forest Meets the Sea,* Jeannie Baker.

- Recognition of the combined power of picture and written text:

  - the pictures adding more degrees of vividness of experience than the words used by themselves (the books of Jeannie Baker);

  - the pictures adding nuances that add extra meaning to the words (the books of Anthony Browne);

  - the pictures being used to reflect characters' fleeting perceptions or memories (*Granpa,* John Burningham);

  - the ways pictures are constructed: the style of the artist/illustrator can impact very strongly on the way the words are 'framed'. Chris Van Allsburg's monochrome cross-hatching is significantly different from the work of Christian Birmingham, or the postmodernist illustrative constructions of Sara Fanelli or Lauren Child. Quentin Blake is wispy and aerie, while Tony Ross and Babette Cole are spiky and uncomfortable. Sophisticated readers should be able to recognise the relationship between words and illustration intended by each book's editor. In that knowledge resides huge understanding of some of the complex ways in which meanings might be made in texts.

- Re-writing 'wordless texts' in 'the style of'…:

  - *The Snowman* by Raymond Briggs offers a very motivating canvas for writers to practise their craft from a number of different perspectives. The picture story sets out the template for the narrative, and then writers supply the actual words. They could, however, be encouraged to write the same story in different 'writerly' styles, based on writers with whom they are familiar. Quentin Blake's *Clown* or some of the texts of David Wiesner, especially *Flotsam,* offer similar opportunities.

Picture books to support literary study

Two really valuable resources for English teachers interested in integrating picture book study in their normal classroom work are:

- Ken Watson (ed) (1997) *Words and Images – Using Picture Books in Years 6 to 10.* Australia: Phoenix Press

- John Stephens, Ken Watson and Judith Parker (2003) *From Picture Book to Literary Theory.* Australia: Phoenix Press

(Both books are available from NATE Publications, Sheffield.)

These stimulating texts, particularly *From Picture Book to Literary Theory*, which is more suited to the age range of English secondary students (the Australians employ a slightly different year group classification), make thoroughly respectable the study of picture books in Key Stage 3 and 4 classrooms. They illustrate how a range of picture books, mostly readily available in English bookshops, can be employed to explore some more demanding aspects about literary learning. *From Picture Book to Literary Theory* adopts a double-page spread for each picture text. The left-hand page comprises a short, valuable essay on an aspect of literary theory: examples include 'social/cultural construction of readers', 'point of view', 'unreliable narrator' and 'intertextuality'. The right-hand page is made up of a number of, mostly, open-ended tasks for students, progressively more demanding in each list, encouraging them to make important insights into the picture book text being considered. The book is also an excellent model on which teachers might like to base their own projects.

This resource could be used at any stage in Key Stage 3, to introduce the study of picture texts to students who might not be familiar with them, or merely to 'warm up' more able students for later more intensive approaches. It could also be used with older students, especially – but not solely – for those who might be intending to move on to university to study literature. It offers a supported and challenging way into a potentially unfamiliar way of 'reading' texts through literary theory, which schools might not have time or the necessary confidence to introduce, but very necessary for modern analysis at university. Teachers could purchase small sets of picture books, for groups of readers to share, or – more interestingly – they could scan the pictures into a computer and project the images of each page on a whiteboard or screen through a PowerPoint or alternative computer program. Seeing the images in that level of detail offers the opportunity for even more intensive analysis.

'Noticing language' in many contexts

A reasonable expectation of more able language users should be that they have an interest in language and a fascination about the ways it works in the many different circumstances it is employed. They should be offered many opportunities to consider language in use at close quarters, and to reflect on how it changes from context to context.

A really simple activity to organise, but one which begins immediate reflection is to conduct a *local language walk*:

1   Take your students on a walk around the local neighbourhood, to study language at work. Shop signs are an interesting starting point, particularly those which attract some creative ideas, such as hairdressers. 'Top Knot', 'Short and Curlies', 'A Cut Above' are all jokey names and need to be appreciated as such. Some cafes and wine bars also try to make an impression through their names.

2   Look at the names of and differences between roads, streets, closes, crescents, walks, lanes, boulevards and so on, and consider their implications. Do they, for instance, point to particular times or events in history, reflect local people or events, or have other significances?

3   Discover any instances of formal language, usually posted by the local council, to announce imminent changes or upgradings of buildings or roads, or warning of demolitions.

4   Find examples of notices and announcements, perhaps outside churches, council offices or some shops.

5   Look out for other examples of street language, on plaques, memorials on wooden benches, possible historical explanations and heritage trail clues.

6   Consider the names and possible backgrounds of the names of cinemas, theatres, clubs and other entertainment sites.

7   Collect different ways of instructing, informing and organising the public, including the word STOP painted on the road surface.

8   Encourage your students to come up with their own categories of language use and support them in probing.

Such an exercise will contribute strongly to students' further knowledge of language, and assist them in 'noticing language' more carefully in other contexts. The same activity, slightly more limited but just as interesting, could just as easily be conducted around the school itself.

Accessing real texts in the world

1   Every student has access to masses of ordinary, everyday texts: pamphlets, catalogues, newspapers, magazines, posters, advertisements and so on. They really are too numerous to list. Encourage more able students to bring in as many bits of information as they can muster, and see how quickly they can build an enormous but diverse collection. There will then be a number of activities that follow: classifying the materials into recognisable types or forms; analysing the intended audiences through the use of particular choices of language; counting the number of word uses; identifying genre; considering how audiences are approached, and so on. As students' familiarity with a growing range of texts increases, so they should be encouraged to raise the different sorts of questions to be asked of them.

2   Students might be invited to make closer connections between the textual materials commissioned or published by different organisations, and how that material relates to the 'representation' or preferred sense of that organisation. So, for example, the television advertisements for the *Sun* newspaper will differ from those for the *Daily Telegraph*, and tell us considerable amounts about the sense, values and ways of seeing the world of the two newspapers. Similarly the advertising flyers for Dell computers will differ considerably from those for Lakeland clothing manufacturers. The audiences, vocabulary, emphases and 'messages' will offer significant comparisons for students to pore over.

3   Compare the front pages of newspapers from different parts of the world. Making a direct comparison between the front pages of the *Sun* and the German daily *Frankfurter Allgemeine,* the French *Le Monde* and the American *Washington Post,* for instance, would raise many questions about their respective world views, about their sense of audience and a huge range of other attitudes to do with class and literacy.

4   Collect a 'series' of advertisements – such as the famous Gold Blend series, or that for Levi's jeans (both campaigns are available on the English and Media Centre *Advertising* resource pack (Grahame 1993), now, unfortunately, out of print but on many English department shelves) – and consider how *representation* of different groups or issues in society is conveyed. So, students might look across a range of advertisements at how children are represented, or young women, or families, or love, or ethnicity, as backgrounds to substantial pieces of study.

5   There are many organisations and professions creating documentation and using language in ways our students might simply not know about. The language of town planning, Ofsted, property conveyancy, or the minutes of formal meetings could be completely unknown territory and worth looking into. Legal documents of different kinds would, of themselves, be rich sources of material, and lend themselves to studying for many reasons. Asking students to attempt to draft a clause for a parliamentary bill would be a taxing and absorbing exercise, pointing to the necessity of precision in language use that they would not normally encounter.

6   The British Library is now easily accessible online and houses a vast collection of texts from different times through history and from many contexts. Their website – www.bl.uk/learning – is the gateway to masses of texts capable of supporting language and literature study of many sorts. As well as making it possible to see examples of writers' original manuscripts, and unusual and unique materials from so many periods of time, there are wonderful links made for projects exploring the changing nature of English through history. In an age when television cooks and cookery programmes are so popular on television, one of the British Library's collections is about texts containing recipes and cookery hints across the ages.

The British Library also has a very impressive collection of voices, sounds and other audio recordings since the invention of the gramophone. New projects are being added all the time, and there will be something of interest for every student's taste. While various projects are already prepared and available, it is also possible to use those on the website as a model for students' own areas of potential research and enquiry. It is, of course, also possible to visit the Library itself, and to arrange with the staff access to materials stored there to support specific and unique projects.

7   Very little detailed study of spoken language ever takes place in schools, unless it is an essential part of an English A level language course. The English teachers' website Teachit (www.teachit.co.uk) contains a number of very supportive and challenging 'modules' created by Tim Shortis and Julie Blake. Able students could be encouraged to set up and follow through straightforward projects designed to study spoken language use in a number of different contexts for themselves. Such a project would be easy to organise and the actual recording of material should not cause too many problems, using modern discreet recording equipment and the sound editing capabilities available in computers. Once again, the British Library could be a further useful resource, as it houses a huge, long-established bank of spoken dialect recordings via the Collect Britain website (www.collectbritain.co.uk/collections/dialects/). From 2007 it is also building a separate collection, called Sounds Familiar, which will include a larger range of voices. Students will be able to access voices from all parts of the British Isles, and listen to the language being spoken from the past, to study how it has changed.

Close reading

George Keith, a former university lecturer in language at Leeds University and a noted examiner, taught me this way of paying utterly close attention to written textual material, which I have adapted and developed. This approach enables students to pay much more careful attention to the way the words resonate, combine and contribute to greater understanding of the full meaning of any text. It is a simple but extremely effective way of introducing new texts to students, but can be used for a range of purposes. It also contributes hugely to students' understanding of how others make meaning, and the literary background resources they draw on, and is a marvellous opportunity for sustained wide-ranging discussion.

Students are expected to read the words of a new text one at a time, or – at most – in a short phrase. As each new word appears, possibly on the page, where students have arranged two pieces of paper to reveal them in a controlled way, or on screen, perhaps on an interactive whiteboard or projected on a light projector, the students are asked to discuss any associations they might bring to the text that has been revealed. I use the opening of Henrietta Branford's rich novel *Fire, Bed and Bone*, or Lesley Howarth's imaginative *Maphead*, as illustrations of the huge numbers of possible ways books can be read, using this approach.

The display for *Fire, Bed and Board* begins with the words 'Chapter One'. As printed in the book, these two words are in an italicised serif style, much like the Times New Roman font, the older fashioned nature of which usually suggests to the students that they are probably reading a text set in the past. The class or group would also be asked to discuss what else they can already assert or suggest about this text, using the full extent of their reading knowledge. More able students usually work out quite quickly that the word 'chapter' eliminates the text being poetry or drama, and it is likely to be prose. They also explain why it is more likely to be fiction, rather than non-fiction (because non-fiction texts invariably include chapter headings, and some indication of the chapter's content), although some remember that chapters of fiction occasionally also have titles or indicators of impending narrative.

After this opening, the first word of the first chapter is revealed – 'The'. Once again they are asked to discuss 'everything they know' about the text slowly unfolding in front of them. After the initial discomfort this request generates, they agree, among other things, that the definite article indicates a specific noun will eventually follow, although it could be preceded by an adjective or two. Through this means, it can be seen, they are also articulating intrinsic linguistic knowledge, which would remain hidden unless brought to light. Following any sharing of ideas and all comment, the next word 'wolves' is revealed. The format for proceeding remains much the same as each word or phrase is focused on: discuss in the groups everything that the students know about texts that refer to wolves. Their knowledge in this topic will be extensive, and good interaction should ensue. Once again, after collaborative de-briefing, the next two words 'came down' are offered to the audience. This time, any speculation is focused on the topography of the setting. The first short paragraph concludes with the wolves speaking: 'to me of freedom'. This sudden and unexpected, and unlikely appearance of an abstract noun is a jolt that simply cannot be replicated in a normal reading of the book. After all this time and attention, in a normal class reading session, readers might well have reached the end of the first chapter. In the way of study recommended here, a mere 15 words have been scrutinised, but the students are already raising more complex and searching questions of the text than they would in the normal reading.

The second short paragraph also concludes with the word 'freedom', with the obvious implication that readers have to take this word very seriously. It demands a high level of respect and attention. In fact, the novel is a study of the Peasants' Revolt, related from the perspective of a dog belonging to the central family of the narrative. So, the word 'freedom' has massive resonance, and the close reading technique ensures that from a very early stage of the reading full cognisance is paid to a central theme.

Further dimensions of understanding and insight can be gained from this approach. Students might be given an envelope, on which they write their names, containing a few pieces of scrap paper. At different stages of the reading they could be invited to date a piece of paper and then predict the likely direction of the narrative, or its ending. As they move through the various events, their views and predictions will change. They might also, at the end of each reading, ask questions of the text, noted down on dated pieces of the scrap paper, which they will expect the text to reveal at a later point.

Of course, after a session or two of this intensive methodology, teachers will then return to the 'normal' pace of reading, otherwise texts would never be completed. But it could well be appropriate to adopt this manner of paying close attention at certain later times in the textual study.

Modern author study

Students in Key Stages 3 and 4 could be offered the opportunity to devise their own areas of study, from lists of admired modern authors. 'Personalisation' has real significance in this context, as students can be given the opportunities to make genuine choices and determine their own routes through this sort of project. The following list is personal and arbitrary, but all the authors I have included have written at least two, and usually many more, novels for young adult readers that have been reviewed very positively from a number of sources:

Vivienne Alcock	David Almond
Malorie Blackman	Tim Bowler
Teresa Breslin	Kevin Brookes
Melvyn Burgess	Ann Cassidy
Robert Cormier	Gillian Cross
Paula Danziger	Peter Dickinson
Berlie Doherty	Anne Fine
Adéle Geras	Alan Gibbons
Morris Gleitzman	Denis Hamley
Sonya Hartnett	Julie Hearne
Nigel Hinton	S. E. Hinton
Anthony Horowitz	Lesley Howarth
Pete Johnson	Geraldine McCaughrean
Michelle Magorian	Margaret Mahy
Jan Mark	Anthony Masters
Michael Murpurgo	Beverley Naidoo
Linda Newbery	Jenny Nimmo
Gary Paulsen	Mal Peet
Philip Pullman	Terry Pratchett
Celia Rees	Meg Rossoff
Louis Sacher	Marcus Sedgewick
Robert Swindells	Jacqueline Wilson

Readers could be encouraged to read all the works by any one of these authors and to consider such features as whether the individual texts bear any relations to each other, either in linguistic, thematic or other ways. Can the reader trace any sorts of development through reading the works of any author in chronological order of publication? What possible dissimilarities might be discovered across the body of work of any single author? Capable readers should be challenged to devise their own areas and topics of study in respect to one or more of these authors. They should certainly be expected to read a number of novels by their selected writer, and really strong readers will read the works of a number of authors. They might then go on to explore and suggest relationships between authors. Which authors work more regularly in which particular genres? Which authors work across a number of genres and are more difficult to pin down?

English teachers should be able to capitalise on this sort of activity by exploiting the knowledge gained as an important dimension of further literary study of classical and more established authors – the sort validated by the school curriculum. All the novels of these authors will necessarily be modern and reflect contemporary preoccupations, interests, mores and cultural references. These issues can be contrasted with similar matters and content of the more traditional canon. Many of the modern texts will be possible to categorise in long-established genres, such as horror, gothic or crime, and students can be prompted to discover the antecedents of such traditions. Others will be new and recently developed, such as magic realism, and students might be invited to consider in what ways those indicators are characterised.

I have long thought that the study of English texts in secondary schools has mostly been conducted the wrong way round. Massive respect is unquestionably afforded to fictional works from the past, and lists of recommended writers have been the staple of the national English curriculum expectation for over a decade. Modern works, particularly those ostensibly written for adolescent readers, are much less well regarded by society at large, government ministers and other influential agencies. Thomas Hardy – good and important; Tim Bowler – entertaining and trivial. Yet these attitudes are culturally determined, and have to do with issues of authority and power, not anything intrinsically part of each work.

Once popular/fashionable texts

Fashioning a course on this topic, as an extension activity for more able readers, is something already under way in at least two schools I know. It can be a very open-ended programme, ranging from exploring why Mary Shelley's *Frankenstein* was such a favourite early in the nineteenth century, through studying the hysteria that surrounded the publication of Charles Dickens' part-works in the middle of the century, causing crowds to line the docks in New York as the latest chapters of *The Old Curiosity Shop* arrived. One department tried to list writers who were once popular, such as Henry Green, whose novels were regarded highly in the mid part of the twentieth century, but are now rarely read.

A recent presentation I observed involved a re-appraisal of texts that had been regarded as important and seminal in the 1950s and 1960s, such as Jack Kerouac's

On the Road, J. D. Salinger's *The Catcher in the Rye,* Robert M. Persig's *Zen and the Art of Motorcycle Maintenance* and Sylvia Plath's *The Bell Jar.* A few very able Year 10 students made some telling commentaries on those times, having also supported their literary studies by looking closely into historical and cultural sources of the times. With the proliferation of DVD versions of films from many periods, it would now be possible for a student to read a text such as one of those named above alongside watching important films from the same historical age: Dennis Hopper's *Easy Rider,* Peter Bogdanovich's *The Last Picture Show,* or Martin Scorsese's *Taxi Driver.*

Cross-over novels

Able readers in the secondary school will not only read the works of those modern authors of books for young people listed above. As they move into Years 9 and 10, their tastes often widen and it is not unusual to find 14- and 15-year-olds reading novels originally published for adults. All the novels in the following list were recommended to me personally in conversation or presentations they made by students between the ages of 14 and 16:

Martin Amis	*London Fields*
Andrea Ashworth	*Once in a House on Fire*
Kate Atkinson	*Behind the Scenes at the Museum*
Margaret Atwood	*Cat's Eye*
Iain Banks	*The Wasp Factory*
Pat Barker	*Regeneration*
A. S. Byatt	*Possession*
Jung Chang	*Wild Swans*
Bruce Chatwin	*On the Black Hill*
Jim Crace	*Quarantine*
Seamus Deane	*Reading in the Dark*
Roddy Doyle	*Paddy Clarke Ha Ha Ha*
Sebastian Faulkes	*Birdsong*
Romesh Gunesekera	*Reef*
David Guterson	*Snow Falling on Cedars*
Nick Hornby	*High Fidelity*

Kazuo Ishiguro	*The Remains of the Day*
Milan Kundera	*The Unbearable Lightness of Being*
Ian McEwan	*The Cement Garden*
Toni Morrison	*Beloved*
Michael Ondaatje	*The English Patient*
Charles T. Powers	*In Memory of the Forest*
E. Annie Proulx	*The Shipping News*
Arundhati Roy	*The God of Small Things*
Vikram Seth	*A Suitable Boy*
Jane Smiley	*A Thousand Acres*
Zadie Smith	*White Teeth*
Dava Sobel	*Longitude*
Graham Swift	*Waterland*
Meera Syal	*Anita and Me*
Jeanette Winterson	*Oranges are not the Only Fruit*

Many of these texts have now been included on A level syllabuses, but these students had discovered them for themselves, or picked up copies their parents were reading. Teachers should be prepared to support readers finding their way into a world of adult writers, and encourage able readers to reach beyond their normal range, when they believe such steps are appropriate.

Works in translation/works from other cultures

We have an extraordinarily rich literary tradition in the United Kingdom, and it would take anybody a very long time to work their way through all the published titles available. Many able students will be guided towards attempting, and we would hope, enjoying texts from the extensive literary canon that helps define this country. Yet there are also equally important collections of fictional, poetic and dramatic works from the rest of the world to know something about. There are a number of important reasons why all students, but certainly more able students, should be encouraged to look carefully at texts from the rest of the world:

• because the texts are important classics in their own right, and many (e.g. Tolstoy's *War and Peace*, Cervantes' *Don Quixote*, Zola's *Germinal*, Ibsen's *The*

Doll's House) would be included on many scholars' lists of the greatest literary works;

- because of what Philip Pullman, in his introduction to the book recommended below (Hallford and Zaghini 2005), calls 'being at home in a strange land': learning about the ways and mores of other peoples;

- because, in an increasingly multi-cultural society, set in an increasingly globalised world, where students in our classes may have backgrounds and roots in more than fifty different ethnic groups, it is important that all our learners should be able freely to access the authentic voices of other cultures and societies.

A good resource to begin focusing on texts from other countries is *Outside In – Children's Books in Translation* by Deborah Hallford and Edgardo Zaghini (2005). To return to an earlier theme, this is a study that would be enhanced by considering the range of picture books from different parts of the world, and comparing them to British publications. But there is also a large group of recommended fiction texts, including works by Cornelia Funke, Daniel Pennac and Jostein Gaarder, who have become better known to British readers during the past decade.

Teachers of secondary English often complain about their students not reading widely enough. More able students, particularly, could be encouraged to interpret 'wide' reading in geographical as well as quantitative terms. They could be challenged or persuaded to include at least one non-UK text in their personalised reading programme, with some background research enabling the student to make a presentation in a shared session.

Contextual study for widening reading

Huge numbers of students study texts such as Steinbeck's *Of Mice and Men* as part of the GCSE English syllabus, and almost as many read *To Kill a Mockingbird* by Harper Lee, but very few use these texts as a springboard for some substantial research into the life and times that produced them. More able students should be invited to explore more widely the conditions and attitudes which prevailed in parts of America in the inter-war years, and discover how other contemporary authors dealt with the same times. Steinbeck himself wrote another classic novel, *The Grapes of Wrath* as well as other works, dealing with the same period, while Scott Fitzgerald, for instance, was dealing with a separate group in the same country in *The Great Gatsby*. But there is also a further group of novels considering America in the same period – works such as Nathanael West's *The Day of the Locust,* set in 1930s Hollywood, or William Faulkner's *Light in August* or *Sanctuary* – which might be enjoyed by some readers. Having read *To Kill a Mockingbird* it would be salutary for an experienced reader to tackle Ralph Ellison's *Invisible Man*.

Similar studies might be planned using DVD film versions of texts. A study of the American 'reluctant hero', for instance, might be conducted through a programme including *Casablanca, Shane, The Man who Shot Liberty Valance, The Magnificent Seven,* and – in a different guise – Robert Mulligan's film version of *To Kill a Mockingbird*.

Unpicking the poetry anthology – literature as a reflection of cultural attitudes and fashions

One resource which many departments are likely to own is an anthology of poetry. Many departments are likely to own more than one anthology, and a few such collections might date back many years. An interesting and challenging exercise for more able readers would be to look closely at examples of anthologies across the ages, and to attempt to draw important conclusions from their findings. They might begin by considering the introductions. To whom are they addressed? Teacher or students? What sorts of values and priorities does the introduction contain? What sorts of assumptions about the reader has the anthology been based on? Do the contents of the anthologies change over time? And then students could probe the answers to these sorts of questions.

Sonnets (or other poetic structures) through time

The sonnet is a clearly defined form of poetry which has been popular in the European traditions of literature for many centuries. Yet there are differences in the form across the years, ranging from the Petrarchan version, and then those by Spenser, Shakespeare and, later, the Romantics, through to modern times. These differences would make a good base for further learning, and encourage a serious literary research project capable of being organised by the students themselves.

The sonnet is not the only possible route to broader learning. The ballad, the ode or the haiku (a really very complex area of poetry, often dealt with rather too superficially in English classrooms) would all make excellent manageable, but challenging areas of study. Comic verse across the centuries would also be an appealing area of interest, while the sturdy and devoted might find the epic poem to be sufficiently testing.

Another activity might be to look out all those poems that deal with the act of writing poetry. They offer different sorts of insight into ways that poets create, and how they feel about the relationship with the works they bring into being. Starting points for this study could be 'Don't ask me' by R. S. Thomas, 'The Thought-fox' by Ted Hughes, and possibly Henry Reed's 'Naming of Parts'.

Texts referring to or working from other texts

A notable characteristic of the postmodern period has been the self-conscious way in which many writers create the material of their own texts either as a response to or in direct reference to other – mostly older – texts. A modern publication by Kurt Brown, *Conversation Pieces: Poems that Talk to Other Poems* (Everyman 2007), presents a number of examples that should cast extra meaning on the original works. U. A. Fanthorpe, with her short selection of four poems, 'Only here for the bier', imagines four of Shakespeare's female characters – Gertrude from *Hamlet*, Emilia from *Othello*, Regan from *King Lear* and the un-named gentlewoman from *Macbeth* – commenting on what she regards as the very masculine world of the plays (*Collected*

Poems 1978–2003, Peterloo Poets 2005). Margaret Atwood wrote a short story, 'Gertrude Talks Back' (*Good Bones and Simple Murders,* Doubleday 1994), in the form of a monologue by Hamlet's mother Gertrude (again), addressing her son with some important extra information. The play *Hamlet* features once more in Wole Soyinka's *Hamlet, or Nigeria's a Prison.* Indeed, possibly the most famous work built on the back of *Hamlet* is *Rosencrantz and Guildenstern are Dead*, by Tom Stoppard. Wendy Cope has established a poetic career using other people's work as the starting point of her own. Another related example in fiction is Jean Rhys's *Wide Sargasso Sea*, which provides the 'back story' to Charlotte Bronte's *Jane Eyre*. Students should be encouraged to make collections of these sorts of texts, seeking out new and different ones for themselves.

Writing tasks

One of the characteristics that will identify a large proportion of more able students is their ability to write fluently and confidently in a number of genres and styles. Some will write for pleasure, possibly short stories and/or poetry, and a few will have aspirations to become writers in their adult lives. Yet again, English teachers will need to be in touch with these talents, supporting and celebrating them appropriately. It is not my intention to state the obvious and say that these writers should be encouraged to practise and develop as well as they are able. Yet, for those who are already accomplished writers, and for a few others who have strong language skills which they may not always manifest in their writing, there are a few tasks that could enable greater attention to the language being employed.

Good writers often enjoy very disciplined exercises, which force them to concentrate on the linguistic features of their efforts. Some very straightforward exercises are based on the following of strict rules, as in the following:

- Writers might try writing a paragraph without using one of the five vowels. (Given this exercise to try and explain The Creation, a teenage writer came up with 'friend of Eve' as a substitute for Adam!)

- Writers have to write a short passage beginning with a one-word sentence, a two-word second sentence, a three-word third sentence, and so on. Having reached, for instance, a nine-word sentence, the writer might then reverse the process.

- Students are asked to write a piece of poetry with a structure like the above, but this time the first word is one syllable; the second line is of two syllables – either a single word, or two single-syllable words; the third line comprises three syllables; and so on. Again, having reached an agreed limit, then reverse the process.

- Write a passage in which the sentences are less than six words long; then try writing the same idea with all sentences over 15 words (these numbers are wholly arbitrary, teachers and students can adjust them, as necessary).

Things for more able English students to do with a rich collection of books

1 Decide what genre(s) each book might be placed in (could be more than one).

2 Make a relationship, with clearly articulated criteria (although *not* similar author), of at least three of this collection of books.

3 Make a relationship, with clearly articulated criteria, with two or three other sorts of texts in other media.

4 Are you able to make a relationship with the book you are reading/have just read from the list, with any of the exam texts/class texts you are studying?

5 Suggest which of the novels might be regarded as 'realistic', and which might be thought of as less 'realistic' (possibly devising a spectrum ranging from one to the other, placing books at different points).

6 State which sorts of modern preoccupations might be noticeable in a selection of these novels (that might not be so obvious, or not at all apparent in books from an earlier period of time).

7 Set yourself the challenge of reading a book that you might usually avoid.

8 Try assessing books in the following sorts of ways:

   • best narrative

   • most effective/unusual use of language

   • most striking use of setting

   • most engaging characters – add other categories for yourself.

9 Read the beginnings of at least five books – and choose one to continue with – and then determine to read to the end, having recorded why you chose that particular text, and what you expect from it.

10 Use the list as a starting point. From it select an author and read the recommended novel, then read at least two more titles by the same author. From this acquaintanceship either write/otherwise prepare a presentation of a modern author study. (Make a set of similarities/ comparisons/contrasts/overlaps etc of your own.)

11 Review books in different styles – e.g. like the *Daily Mail* book page/the *Guardian* Saturday Review section/the review page of a contemporary young women's magazine – and other styles you can find.

12 Make a collection of already published reviews of your chosen novel, from a range of sources – and comment on them, agreeing or otherwise.

13 Write or make a presentation of a claim for your chosen novel to be included in the Carnegie Book Awards shortlist.

14 Set out a series of bullet points to:

- a parent

- a teacher

- other students

- a librarian

- a governor

to convince them that your novel should be included in your school library.

15 Select any *three* things about the book you are reading that you found particularly significant.

16 Prepare a short programme of activities/learning focuses you would be prepared to employ if you were teaching your novel as a class text.

17 Set up a group of three or four students, who have all nominated different favourite reads from the recommended list – and conduct a 'balloon debate' in front of the class, to see which book remains as the eventual winner.

18 Talk about at least one of the books from the list with another student, recommending why they should give it a try.

19 Encourage at least one adult to read a book you enjoyed and find the opportunity to have a conversation with them about it.

20 Listen to a book-based programme on Radio 4 – such as 'Open Book' and prepare a short item in the style of one section of the programme about two or three novels you have read. Try recording it.

- Agree on a standard formula, such as the following 'four sentence' model I have regularly used in a number of circumstances. This particular example is based on a perfect example of the 'recount' genre: in the past tense, in chronological order, first or third person active voice, employing words or phrases of chronology as connectives. It begins with orientation (answering the 5 'W' questions), proceeds through simple developing events, and ends with re-orientation, or a conclusion. This one has three simple sentences and one compound sentence. An example might be:

'Last week we went on a bus to the theatre in London. The play was very clever. We all enjoyed the experience and thought it would be helpful for our revision. It was a worthwhile trip.' Based on the same model, students now write their own recount – real or imagined, serious or amusing.

Having established a standard template, they could then be invited to add or remove specific features to it: e.g. add any word to each sentence not an adjective; turn all the sentences into compound sentences; make every part of the passage negative in tone; add an explanatory phrase to two sentences, and so on. Students should be encouraged to come up with their own amendments or changes, and consider the implications of any adaptations made.

- Attempt to write a continuing narrative in a variety of text types – a letter, a newspaper report, a non-fiction text, a poem, a diary, a legal document, a report, and so on. Or write a narrative in a mixture of writing genres.

- Write a passage for a particular purpose, but analyse a portion of the piece very carefully in grammatical terms, by, perhaps, using different coloured type on a computer, different fonts representing, for instance, different word classes, or by employing coloured marker pens to indicate different linguistic devices. In this exercise able writers should begin to apply a careful self-evaluation of their own style and techniques, and – possibly – make some adjustments to improve their work.

- Pastiche: each week (currently, on a Tuesday) the *Guardian* publishes the Digested Read, a column devoted to a review of a newly published book, in the style of the book (John Crace, *Digested Read*, Atlantic 2005). Students might like to write in that manner about a book or other suitable publication. Often schools ask students to write book reviews; more able students could write reviews of books, or television or films, in the style of critics in, for instance, the *Daily Mail* or currently popular young women's magazines: *Twist, Seventeen* or *Cosmo Girl*.

Science fiction from all angles: an example of a genre study

A considerable number of able boys (and quite a lot of girls) enjoy science fiction in one form or another. This is another category of narrative that would benefit from a multi-modal approach. Students who read this sort of fiction might be persuaded to look at the earliest works in the genre – possibly Mary Shelley's *Frankenstein* – but certainly such titles as *Journey to the Centre of the Earth* by Jules Verne or *The Time Machine* by H. G. Wells. The differences between those texts and modern science fiction could be a good starting point for study. Students should be challenged into thinking about why science fiction became a popular genre at a particular point in history, and the sensibilities that drove it.

There is a massive back catalogue of science fiction films, most of it still available for viewing on DVD. While yet again being encouraged to compare the modern sci-fi films with those of an earlier time (Georges Méliès trick photographic *Le Voyage dans la Lune* is a notable example), more able students might also be invited to think about different sub-genres of science fiction. Science fiction films are capable of being interpreted (that is, 'read') in at least the following five ways:

- **'Space operas'**: like soap operas – where human problems are taken to the far flung stars! (Possible examples: *2001, A Space Odyssey*; *Forbidden Planet*; *Solaris*; *Silent Running*; *Star Wars*.)

- **Dystopias**: grim eventualities have come to be our ruling forces, usually the punishment for some major ethical laxness. (Possible examples: *Metropolis*; *1984*; *Westworld*; *The Truman Show*; *Blade Runner*; *THX-1138*; *The Terminator*.)

- **Earth in peril**: we're under attack from some menacing force! (Possible examples: *Invasion of the Body Snatchers*; *The Day the Earth Stood Still*; *Armageddon*; *Close Encounters of the Third Kind*.)

- **Science out of control**: the arrogance of mankind has got beyond itself. (Possible examples: *Jurassic Park*; *The Invisible Man*; *The Fly*; *28 Days Later*; *Coma*.)

- **Cyberpunk** – we are really a virtual world. (Possible examples: *Tron*; *The Matrix*; *Minority Report*; *Videodrome*.)

Students should be urged to consider the times in which these films and the books on which they were based were released, or written. Links might then be made between, for instance, the anti-communist paranoia in the USA in the early 1950s, and the popularity of *The Day the Earth Stood Still* and *Invasion of the Body Snatchers*. Similarly, perceptive readers will be aware of the disillusionments of the late 1970s/ early 1980s being a suitable context for a film such as *Blade Runner*. Most students researching in this area will also be acutely aware of the considerable continuing improvements in film-making special effects, which has made films such as *Jurassic Park* and *The Matrix* possible. True devotees will also include a consideration of television programmes, such as *Dr Who* in its earlier and modern manifestations, and other formerly seminal productions, such as the various *Quatermass* films. There might even be those who try to gain a sense of the terror unleashed by Orson Welles, in his *War of the Worlds* 1938 radio broadcast, which is, of course, to be found on the internet: http://members.aol.com/jeff1070/script.html.

Similar sorts of study could be devised for the crime/epic/western/film noir/other genres.

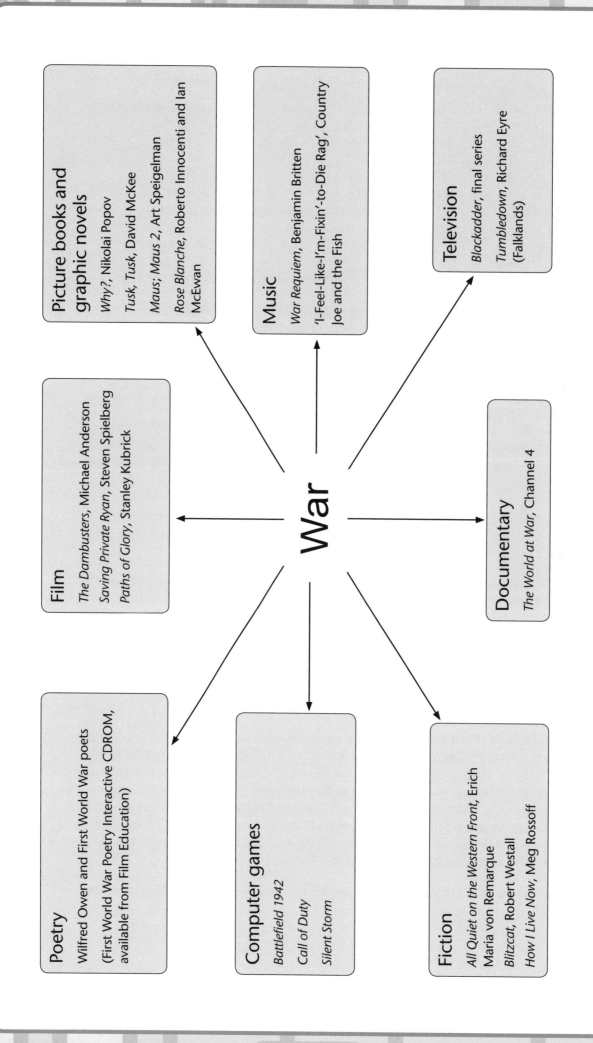

Poetry

Wilfred Owen and First World War poets

(First World War Poetry Interactive CDROM, available from Film Education)

Computer games

Battlefield 1942

Call of Duty

Silent Storm

Fiction

All Quiet on the Western Front, Erich Maria von Remarque

Blitzcat, Robert Westall

How I Live Now, Meg Rossoff

Film

The Dambusters, Michael Anderson

Saving Private Ryan, Steven Spielberg

Paths of Glory, Stanley Kubrick

War

Picture books and graphic novels

Why?, Nikolai Popov

Tusk, Tusk, David McKee

Maus; Maus 2, Art Speigelman

Rose Blanche, Roberto Innocenti and Ian McEwan

Music

War Requiem, Benjamin Britten

'I-Feel-Like-I'm-Fixin'-to-Die Rag', Country Joe and the Fish

Television

Blackadder, final series

Tumbledown, Richard Eyre (Falklands)

Documentary

The World at War, Channel 4

Radio

There is almost no study of radio in schools, yet radio is increasingly popular in society generally. The BBC broadcasts over 600 hours of drama a year but little is heard in classrooms. A number of important plays have been broadcast over the years and many use the imaginative power of sound very successfully. In many respects radio is a medium that allows a writer to do anything and go absolutely anywhere. More able students might be interested to explore the differences between the television and film versions of Douglas Adams' *The Hitchhiker's Guide to the Universe* and its original radio incarnation. They will soon realise how much more scope is possible in circumstances where that audience is able to imagine the mental pictures of what they are hearing, rather than depending on set designers attempting to bring to the screen much less creditable versions of the same idea. Students might be encouraged to listen to Lee Hall's powerful radio play *Spoonface Steinberg* (obtainable from the BBC CD library), of a young child's musings, as she stoically prepares for death from cancer. They could discuss what their different reactions would be if they were able to watch a television version of this play. In the same way, they could actually compare very easily the radio and televised versions of Alan Bennett's *Talking Heads* playlets.

With sophisticated audio computer programs becoming readily available, the imaginative student has that possibility of thinking in all sorts of directions and dimensions, simply not possible in fully realised visual worlds. Students could be encouraged to write monologues, for instance, or to employ layers of sound, in much the same way that they might build up a fabricated picture in Photoshop. This sort of exercise has the advantages of fulfilling many creative objectives, as well as adding to the stock of a student's technological skills.

Radio also presents a range of possible spoken activities, not all of them necessarily formal. Young people are less used to talk radio, usually tuning to musical stations, but they could be encouraged to take part in recorded discussions, with some editing of what has been said. They might undertake more formal presentations, making short talks of textual reviews or other suitable curriculum-related topics. A number of schools have invested in school radio stations, where loudspeakers placed strategically around the school gather interested listeners. Fashioning different sorts of talk for different audiences and contexts would offer a valuable platform for learning more about oral language skills.

IT skills

Anything recommended in this book, published in the early part of the twenty-first century, is not likely to have a very long shelf life. Technology is developing too quickly for anything more than a snapshot of worthwhile activities to be mentioned at this moment, before it goes quickly out of date. So only a few general ways in which ICT might be deployed are included below:

1   Computer technology offers the opportunity for all sorts of playful activity with written language. Working very straightforwardly in Word enables students to

move text around with great ease, to change the colour, size, style and other features of different fonts and to make a large range of presentational choices. Writers will be able to explore a number of possibilities of meanings, and make decisions about which final configuration best suits the overall intended meaning, or what happens to meanings when particular textual combinations are at work.

2   Programs like Photoshop enable students to make an almost limitless number of new illustrative texts. Photographs can be combined in creative and extraordinary ways to bring about situations that could never happen naturally. Pictures scanned into the computer from virtually any source can be amended and played with in every imaginable way. Superb illustrations can be constructed to accompany written material, or combined into slide presentations, possibly with music and spoken commentary.

3   Moving-image technologies now enable students to make films of a very high quality. A number of affordable edit programs are available, such as Adobe Premiere, but anybody with reasonable access to a modern PC will find an edit facility as part of the natural built-in toolkit. Students at Parkside College in Cambridge find fascinating a feature of their curriculum which encourages them to re-edit professional commercial films, to explore other alternative ways in which the director might have made similar or parallel meanings.

A project I have recently seen working very effectively has involved students collecting appropriate visual imagery, moving and still, to accompany readings of poetry. Work such as this not only provides a good indication of the meanings these particular students have developed about the works they are studying, but it has also served as useful reference points for students who have experienced difficulty gaining a hold on the poems.

4   IT allows students to store huge sections of moving-image texts from many different sources. A reasonably sized hard disk on most computers (or separate hard disk with storage of anything up to 500GB currently available) can hold very large numbers of full length films. With this kind of facility students and teachers can readily access selections of texts – such as scenes from Shakespeare plays – from a number of different productions, and can rapidly make informed comparisons of the various elements of each production. This sort of ease of access was never available before. Those studying these extracts can focus intensely on the material: playing, pausing and replaying with no time-wasting.

Further reading

Ken Watson (ed) (1997) *Words and Images – Using Picture Books in Years 6 to 10*. Australia: St Clair Press.

John Stephens, Ken Watson and Judith Parker (eds) (2003) *From Picture Book to Literary Theory*. Australia: St Clair Press.

Deborah Hallford and Edgardo Zaghini (2005) *Outside In – Children's Books in Translation*. Chicago: Milet.

References

Atwood, Margaret (1994) 'Gertrude talks back', in *Good Bones and Simple Murders*. New York: Doubleday, pp. 16–19.

Bennett, David (2001) *The School of the Future: Key Issues for School Leaders*. Nottingham: NCSL.

Betts, G.T. and J. K. Kercher (1999) *Autonomous Learner Model: Optimizing Ability*. Greeley, CO: ALPS Publishing.

Betts, G.T. and J. Knapp (1981) 'The autonomous learner model: a secondary model'. In *Secondary Programs for the Gifted and Talented*, ed. A. Arnold. Los Angeles, CA: National/State Leadership Training Institute for the Gifted and Talented.

Bloom, B. S. (ed) (1956) *Taxonomy of Educational Objectives: The Classification of Educational Goals*. Susan Fauer Company, Inc.; pp. 201–7.

Bowring-Carr, Christopher and John West-Burnham (1997) *Effective Learning in Schools*. London: Pearson Education.

Branford, Henrietta (1997) *Fire, Bed and Board*. London: Walker Books.

Brown, Kurt (2007) *Conversation Pieces: Poems that Talk to Other Poems*. London: Everyman's Library Pocket Poets.

Clarke, Shirley (2003) *Enriching Feedback in the Primary Classroom*. London: Hodder & Stoughton.

Cliff Hodges, Gabrielle (2006) 'The Four Cs and Other Letters of the Alphabet – English 21 and the Future of English'. *EnglishDramaMedia,* January, Issue 5: pp. 5–6.

Cox, Brian (1991) *Cox on Cox: An English Curriculum for the 1990s*. London: Hodder & Stoughton.

Dean, Geoff (2004) *Improving Learning in English*. London: David Fulton.

DfEE (2001) *Key Stage 3 National Strategy – Framework for Teaching English: Years 7, 8 and 9*. London: DfEE.

DfEE/QCA (1999) *English: The National Curriculum for England*. London: QCA.

Eagleton, Terry (1983) *Literary Theory: An Introduction*. Oxford: Blackwell.

Fanthorpe, U. A. (2005) *Collected Poems 1978–2003*. Cornwall: Peterloo Poets.

Frater, Graham (1993) 'Back to the Future'. *Education,* 22 January: p. 51.

Galton, M., J. Gray and J. Ruddock (2003) *Transfer and Transitions in the Middle Years of Schooling (7–14): Continuities and Discontinuities in Learning.* University of Cambridge Research Report No. 443.

Gilbert, Christine (chair) *2020 Vision.* Report of the Teaching and Learning in 2020 Review Group. DfES, December.

Goodwyn, Andrew (1999) 'The Cox Models Re-visited: English teachers' views of their subject and the National Curriculum'. *English in Education,* 33 (2), Summer: pp. 19–31.

Goodwyn, Andrew (ed) (2000) *English in the Digital Age.* London: Cassell.

Goodwyn, Andrew (2004) 'Literacy versus English? A Professional Identity Crisis'. Paper to NATE Conference, January.

Grahame, Jenny (1993) *Advertising.* London: English and Media Centre.

Hallam, Susan (2002) *Ability Grouping in Schools.* London: Institute of Education.

Hallford, Deborah and Edgardo Zaghini (2005) *Outside In – Children's Books in Translation.* Chicago: Milet.

Hargreaves, D. (2005) *Personalising Learning 3: Learning to Learn and the New Technologies.* London, INet/ Specialist Schools Trust. www.clusterweb.org.uk/docs/HargreavesPersonalisedLearning.pdf

Howarth, Lesley (1994) *Maphead.* London: Walker Books.

Marsden, J. and S. Tan (1998) *The Rabbits.* Melbourne: Lothian Books.

Miliband, David (2004) 'Choice and Voice in Personalised Learning'. DfES Innovation Unit/DEMOS/OECD conference, London, 18 May.

Moore, Alan and Dave Gibbons (1986/87) *Watchmen.* New York: Titan Books.

Paule, M. (2006) 'Gifted Identities in Popular Culture – or what Clark Kent could learn from TV'. *EnglishDramaMedia* (Sheffield: NATE), January: pp. 7–11.

Prensky, Marc (2005/2006) 'Learning in the digital age'. *Educational Leadership,* 63 (4), Dec/Jan: pp. 8-13. Online at http://www.ascd.org/authors/ed_lead/el200512_prensky.html.

Renzulli, J. S. (1997) 'Five dimensions of differentiation'. Keynote presentation at the 20th Annual Confratute Conference, Storrs, CT.

Scholes, R. (1998) *The Rise and Fall of English: Restructuring English as a Discipline.* New Haven & London: Yale University Press.

Slavin, R. E. (1990) 'Achievement effects of ability grouping in secondary schools: a best evidence synthesis'. *Review of Educational Research,* 60: pp. 471–90.

Spiegelman, Art (1986) *Maus 1.* New York: Pantheon Books.

Spiegelman, Art (1991) *Maus 2.* New York: Pantheon Books.

Stephens, John, Ken Watson and Judith Parker (eds) (2003) *From Picture Book to Literary Theory*. Sydney: St Clair Press.

Thomas, Peter (2007) 'A question of challenge 1'. *The Secondary English Magazine,* February: pp. 21–4.

Tomlinson, C. A. (1995). *How to differentiate instruction in mixed-ability classrooms.* Alexandria, VA: Association for Supervision and Curriculum Development.

Watson, Ken (ed) (1997) *Words and Images – Using Picture Books in Years 6 to 10.* Australia: St Clair Press.

Wiliam, Dylan and Paul Black (1998) *Inside the Black Box: Raising Standards through Classroom Assessment.* London: King's College, London.

Index